'A lucid and inspiring ... base camp. This is a book about friendship, ... camaraderie, about believing in one another. But eventually it is about believing in oneself and of the mind's ability to control the body and conquer a mountain.'

—**Vikas Swarup**
Author and High Commissioner of India to Canada

'A mountain represents an obstacle and an opportunity. We need to search out the mountains in our life and find a way to climb them. We conquer them not in a physical way but really in our minds. The difference is in the way they present themselves to us—do we search them out, or do they present themselves to us. Hari, has always been a fighter and a person of great resilience. The way he has set out the book offers us a ready way to win our battles at our terms and in a seamless way.

2905 is an important number. It is 29th May, the day Everest was conquered. Each year it reminds me of what two men can do once they set their minds on something. It also tells me that nothing is impossible. It was not a physical act but a mental feat. Hari's book is very inspiring, for it asks you to search for some meaning in your life, a goal and find a way to reach it.'

—**S.V. Nathan**
Partner and Chief Talent Officer, Deloitte India

MIND OVER MOUNTAIN

A CORPORATE LEADER'S JOURNEY

HARI KUMAR

Konark Publishers Pvt. Ltd
206, First Floor,
Peacock Lane, Shahpur Jat,
New Delhi110 049
Phone: +91-11-41055065, 65254972
e-mail: india@konarkpublishers.com
website: www.konarkpublishers.com

Konark Publishers International
1507 Western Avenue, #605,
Seattle, WA 98101
Phone: (415) 409-9988
e-mail: us@konarkpublishers.com

Cataloging in Publication Data--DK

Courtesy: D.K. Agencies (P) Ltd. <docinfo@dkagencies.com>

Kumar, Hari (Entrepreneur), author.
    Mind over mountain : a corporate leader's journey / Hari Kumar.
    pages cm
    ISBN 9789322008796

    1. Mountaineering--Everest, Mount (China and Nepal) 2. Everest,
Mount (China and Nepal)--Description and travel. 3. Kumar, Hari
(Entrepreneur)--Travel--Everest, Mount (China and Nepal) 4. Executives-
-Travel--Everest, Mount (China and Nepal)   I. Title.

LCC GV199.44.E85K86 2018 I DDC 796.522095496   23

Editors: Dipali Singh and Seetha Natesh
Cover and book design by Misha Oberoi
Typeset by 3P Solutions, New Delhi
Printed and bound at Thomson Press (India) Ltd.

To my family and those close friends who made this book possible—thanks for your constant support and for putting up with me. Most importantly—thanks for believing in me more than I believe in myself every single day.

To Phakdin Two (TJ!), the 'super duper nag' who made me finish writing this book, kudos! (Boy, can he be a real nag!).

To my friends who were the first to read/edit the manuscript and say, 'I love it. I enjoyed it. Now change it.' Thank you!

To those who constantly discourage me, thanks for the motivation and those who are constantly jealous of me. Get a life!

To my fellow Phakdins. We did it! Thanks for making it happen! Love you all.

To everyone else, look at all problems straight in the eye and say Just Ding it!!!

In one of the worst avalanches on Mount Everest on 18 April 2014, sixteen Sherpas (mountaineers) died. They were right behind our group as we had come down from the Everest Base Camp by then—we missed the avalanche by just nine days. My prayers go out to each of them and their families.

The Sherpas are the true heroes on the mountains. They work hard each day with a positive attitude and help others to succeed. They are the heroes who selflessly put themselves out there for trekkers and climbers to feel safe and get a sense of achievement. To each of them and their families, THANK YOU!

'It is not the mountain that I conquered, it is myself'.

—SIR EDMUND HILLARY

CONTENTS

FOREWORD

I met Hari over 10 years ago as a young partner in the firm. Like most partners, he is smart, confident and extremely hard working with a 'never give up' attitude. Over the decade that I have known him, it has been wonderful to see him grow into an inspirational and progressive leader.

As the CEO of the US firm and subsequently the global CEO, I got to see Hari very closely. He was always open-minded and his commitment to the job unquestionable. His large heart and extremely caring attitude towards his people made him unique.

Seeing him work at the pace that he did, I was worried. I knew he would burn out quick and I did warn him several times. So, I was shocked, but not surprised, when in February 2012, I was informed that he was paralysed and could not move.

I knew that if there was anyone that could fight and recover, it would be him. Several months later, when I visited his city, he had started to walk. It was obvious to me that he was still in pain but he did not let on. He wanted to make sure that my trip was successful and worked on all arrangements and even came to meet me. That's the kind of fellow Hari is!

In this book, I read how a strong young leader's life was changed overnight. In that moment of adversity, he realized what priorities in life truly mean and how we, in the corporate world, often tend to forget to 'stop and smell the roses'.

He has not given any formal advice in this book. Yet, through his experience, he makes each one of us stop and think—What are the true moments that matter in life? The narrative style is no different than his character—straight from the heart. It keeps the reader engrossed and enthralled.

My congratulations to Hari on this book! I wish him all success.

Barry Salzberg
Retired CEO,
Deloitte, LLP

PROLOGUE

From being paralysed and helpless, lying in the hospital gurney to the top of the Everest Base Camp...

I lay on my hospital bed, staring at the white ceiling. The sounds of doctors and nurses scurrying around attending to patients in the Emergency room were muted in my head. All I could see, hear and sense was my entire life flashing before me.

I was in the prime of my youth—active and driven by the attitude that I had plenty to achieve in this lifetime. I was the go-getter who worked sixteen hours a day to stay ahead in the corporate rat race. For me, rising to become a partner at one of the world's largest and prestigious firms at age twenty-nine (about ten years earlier than most others) was not sufficient. I considered coming in second an abject failure. 'What next?' was always the question for me, while 'stop and smell the roses' was a phrase best left for losers.

I AM NOT STAYING IN BED FOR THE REST OF MY LIFE. WHATEVER THE CAUSE IS, I'LL FIGHT MY WAY OUT OF PARALYSIS

Until two hours ago, I had been all that. Successful, accomplished, and confident. Now I was lying in a hospital bed with all my cognitive abilities intact, but with my right side paralysed. My right hand and leg would not move. Fortunately, a heavy cocktail of painkillers relieved my pain.

I was in the denial stage of the five phases of tragedy. Random thoughts were whizzing through my cerebral cortex. 'This cannot be happening to me. I was fine a few hours ago. Oh God! Why me? What have I done wrong? I cannot afford to spend the rest of my life in bed. What if I die in this state?' My flair for dramatization was not lost in my moment of despair.

As there had been no preceding trauma, the initial prognosis was a massive heart attack resulting in radiating pain and internal bleeding. But it had been over two hours since I first experienced pain. Don't heart attacks kill within minutes? The ECG results came in and ruled out the possibility of a myocardial infarction to my great relief. The next course of tests included an X-ray so I was wheeled into the X-ray room.

As I lay on the cold flat steel of the X-ray table, feeling helpless, the realization of the frailty of life dawned on me. One moment, everything had been perfect, but in the next, my life had been turned upside down.

Lying on that hospital bed, paralysed and helpless, I promised myself, 'I am not staying in bed for the rest of my life. Whatever the cause is, I'll fight my way out of paralysis.' A thought whizzed through my mind, giving me a shred of hope to cling on to, to live for. It was a promise to myself, 'I will regain my strength and trek up the tallest mountain in the world—nothing less than Mount Everest.'

ONE

HIM KA AALAY
The playground of the gods

HIMALAYA ('HIM KA AALAY')—the ultimate destination. 'Himalaya' is a Sanskrit word that means the abode or temple of snow. Scaling this mountain is a true test of character, determination, and the desire to explore the unknown. So pristine, untouched, and beautiful—it certainly is the playground for the gods.

Ancient Hindu texts tell you that you could not do justice to the Himalayas even in 'a hundred years of the gods' or millions of years of a human life. If that is truly the case, should we mortals even make the attempt to do so?

The youngest and highest mountain range in the world, the Himalayas extend from Kyrgyzstan in the west to Myanmar in the east, and spread over a distance of 4,000 kilometres. That is to say, it is spread over an area that is over ten times the size of France and has over 100 mountains that are over 23,622 feet (7,200 metres) in height. This mountain range can claim almost all the superlatives for itself—tallest mountains, deepest gorges, steepest cliffs, heaviest snow, greatest biodiversity in the world. Separating the Indian subcontinent in the south from the Tibetan plateau in the north, the Himalayas are the source for many of the largest rivers in the world that have given birth to the oldest human civilizations.

SO PRISTINE, UNTOUCHED, AND BEAUTIFUL— IT CERTAINLY IS THE PLAYGROUND OF THE GODS

Geologically these mountains are 50 million years old and hence relatively young. At 29,028 feet (8,848 metres), Mount Everest is the highest mountain in the world and certainly grabs the lion's share of global attention. But the Himalayas have thirteen other mountains over 26,000 feet (8,000 metres) high. Avid mountaineers call it the Grand Slam of mountain climbing if you make it to the top of all fourteen.

The Everest Base Camp

Located on the edge of the Khumbu ice fall that originates at the summit of the mountain, and at a height of approximately 18,500 feet (5,400 metres), is the Everest Base Camp (EBC). The first and main camp set up to fully acclimatize mountaineers in their attempt to reach the summit of Mount Everest, it is where the trek ends for amateur mountaineers and begins for professionals. Nestled in the Sagarmatha National park, the EBC is understandably the most popular trek destination in the area.

TWO

THE PROMISE

THERE WAS NOT A LOT TO DO as I lay in the hospital bed. The IV needle in my left hand meant I couldn't move it around and my right hand was uncooperative as it was paralysed. So nothing was moving in my body other than the constant flood of thoughts in my brain.

In the limited arc of my sight due to the restricted motion of my neck, I watched the nurses going about their business and thought about the acute pressure these professionals face all day, working within the few minutes that separate life and death for a human being.

The painkillers were taking effect and I was in a state between sleep and wakefulness. I was caught in a conflict of emotions. Acute pain, moderated by medicines, panic, and the fear that I would spend the rest of my life in bed battled the determination to recover.

As I lay there, my mind started to wander. For a long time, the mountains and stories of the endurance and determination of people who had conquered them had fascinated me. As the tallest and most majestic, Mount Everest was the ultimate pinnacle. *Life is what happens when you are busy planning it*—and this could not be truer in my case. I wondered if 1 would get a chance to fulfil my dream.

Like most modern corporate professionals, I had often considered taking time off to climb the mountains, dive in the oceans, serve the underprivileged, and make a meaningful difference to my own life and that of others. But like most modern corporate professionals, these grand plans had the most flexible deadlines, so never saw the light of day. When all else failed, there was always the big daddy of excuses—if I leave my job for an extended period, the whole office would crash. It was a false sense of being indispensable.

Just as I was drifting off, there was a lot of noise around me. I opened my eyes to see several doctors in white coats standing around my bed talking. I wasn't sure if they were talking to me. The medicines were still quite potent, and while I could hear what they said, I could only comprehend some parts of it. I heard the words 'cervical discs', 'slip', 'rehab', and a whole lot of what seemed gibberish. I slipped back into sleep and when I woke up, I was staring into the eyes of my personal doctor who had come to the Emergency room on hearing that I was there.

'How are you doing?' he asked.

'Feeling a lot better, Doctor,' I said. 'What happened? Do you know?'

'The good news is that your condition is not life-threatening. The not-so-good-news is that three of your cervical discs have slipped. Seeing that you did not go through a trauma, it must have been caused by your excessive travel and stress. I have always told you to take it easy. The mad race is not worth it.'

'So what happens now?' I asked.

'You feel paralysed because the body is preventing any further degradation of the condition. It is an automatic reaction of the human body. But there's no permanent nerve damage, and I believe you will regain sensation. However, I must tell you there is no guarantee. Unfortunately, this could take weeks or months of rehab. But we will wait for the orthopaedic surgeon to confirm.'

It was the best news I had heard. There was hope! On the one hand, I was relieved, but on the other, fearful because my doctor was not sure about when I would fully recover. Why do doctors always tell us about the probability of this or the likelihood of that? Don't they understand that we need reassurance? What I needed was for him to be God and tell me I would be all right, that I could walk out of the hospital in the next few minutes. I cried myself to sleep, but the panic woke me again. Desperately, I started asking anyone who would talk to me if I would be okay—the attending doctors, the nurses, and even the orderlies.

In response to my panic-driven queries, someone messaged my orthopaedic surgeon to let him know I was awake. After what seemed like an eternity, but was only about twenty-five minutes in reality, he came over. He told me that I would never be a 100 per cent fit, but that I could have almost all my life back if I worked at it. He said the path would be long, tedious, and painful.

His words were reassuring. I did not want to hear anything beyond 'You can have almost all your life back'. I was not going to spend the rest of my life in bed.

The weeks and months that followed in daily rehab were some of the most painful ones of my life. I met many orthopaedic doctors for second opinions and got third opinions. The general consensus was that

YOU CAN HAVE ALMOST ALL YOUR LIFE BACK I WONDER IF IT WAS DETERMINATION DRIVEN BY THE STRENGTH OF MY CHARACTER OR SIMPLY THE SHEER MAGNITUDE OF MY DESPERATION. IT HAD TAKEN A MAJOR INCIDENT LIKE PARALYSIS TO HELP ME REALIZE WHAT MATTERS IN LIFE.

surgery was too dangerous unless I became totally debilitated and could not move. They told me that the five-year results of the surgical or non-surgical option were more or less the same. In short, the prognosis was 'Live with it. Learn to manage the pain.'

To me, there are two broad categories of successful people in the world—those for whom success seems guaranteed and those who have to work hard and hope they catch a break once in a while. As a person, I am goal-oriented and determined. I believe that I belong to the second type of successful people. I am seldom at the right place at the right time and have to make an effort of 150 per cent to succeed. But I still deem myself lucky since I do taste success as a result of hard work.

Most of us take much for granted in our daily lives, such as the basic ability to walk and run. Over those days, weeks, and months of my illness, I was taken decades back to my infancy. I had to re-learn to stand up and as the cliché goes 'learn to crawl and walk before I could run'. There was a new meaning to the words 'baby steps'. Like when I was a baby, I tried and tried and failed. Those days of rehab have been the most tearful in my life, a result of both the sheer physical pain and the emotional rollercoaster I experienced.

As I continued the fight on the path to learning to walk, the positive part was that my determination to combat the odds did not waver. As I look back, I wonder if it was determination driven by the strength of my character or simply the sheer magnitude of my desperation.

It was not a journey to getting back to normality. It was a journey of learning to adapt to the new reality and making the best of it. The early days were the toughest. I could not do anything on my own, needing help just to sit up in bed or step into the bathroom.

Days became weeks and weeks became months. I was not improving. The desperation was slowly becoming acceptance. Every day was a constant fight to motivate myself not to give up. The only thing that kept me going was 'attitude'. I refused to accept that this was a permanent condition.

As the word spread, recommendations and suggestions for recovery and pain alleviation poured in from friends, family, and even strangers and still do to this day.

Many people believe they are the experts in back pain. I suppose almost everyone has experienced it in their daily lives, and they feel they can relate to it, but no one really understood the gravity of my condition. I had recommendations for—and against—yoga, allopathy, homeopathy, Ayurveda, and acupuncture as well as names of dozens of experts and specialists. Books, magazines, white papers—I read almost everything on this subject and tried almost every possible method to alleviate the pain, as long as it wasn't intrusive or meant introducing a foreign substance into my body.

In the hospital, at the height of my panic, I had promised myself that I would climb to the EBC. That was a goal that gave me the impetus to work hard through rehab to fully recover. My passion for the outdoors, combined with my deterministic attitude, kept pushing me forward.

After I had consulted many doctors, I settled on an orthopaedic surgeon who seemed the most practical and understood my predicament. While I was not sure it was the right thing to do, he had urged me to set my own limits of tolerance. He wanted me to push myself till I could do so no more—physically and through the pain. Most of the advice I had received so far was advocating bed rest and limiting my movements only to physiotherapy. This doctor's words, naturally, sounded the best to my ears.

Overall, this seemed like my relationship with astrologers or tarot card readers—if you talk to several of them, you can always get the answer you want.

The early steps were painful. I stuck to just the exercises that the doctor recommended to strengthen my muscles. Even that was not easy. Over a few days and weeks, I started feeling more confident doing the basic exercises and soon the competitor in me took over. I started setting new goals for myself on a weekly basis and pushed hard through the pain to get to them. Goals ranged from the amount of time spent exercising to specific ones targeting muscles that would allow me to move my hands or legs again.

I made the goals aggressive but realistic. The 'wins' or 'successes' helped to motivate me even further—

but the pain grew as well. I still continued to remain determined, which strengthened my tolerance to pain.

Every step was a wonderful journey towards discovering myself. As a child, one does not have the ability to comprehend this. As an adult, it was wonderful to be 'growing', developing basic movements and motion. I was watching myself grow through the phases of infancy into childhood and adulthood. With each success, my confidence grew and after months of not giving up, one day, I managed to stand upright without support.

That was a momentous occasion. Like a child, I fell several times. But I never hesitated to make myself stand again. I guess the infant in me helped to squash the fear of failure. With each step, I was even more determined to get back up. I began walking a few steps and over a few weeks, was walking indoors—and then, I developed enough courage to walk outdoors.

Each time I pushed further, the pain got worse and I had to endure a day or two of intense pain. Fighting through it, I extended my walks to almost an hour a day. I added swimming to the agenda and followed the same process. I had to learn to swim all over again. As my hands and legs started to slowly come back under my control in a limited manner, I started jogging in the mornings and swimming in the late afternoons.

Each day that I could tolerate the pain, I continued to exercise—walk, jog, swim, and then run.

The pain—and my determination to overcome it—did wonderful things. It changed my lifestyle; it made me focus on my health and my body. Until my hospitalization, I'd been far too busy to take time out for these important aspects. Now, my priorities had changed, and miraculously, there was time to do it.

So there was, after all, something positive that came out of my plight. It had taken a major incident like paralysis to help me realize what matters in life.

A year and half had passed since I had woken up paralysed. I had regained much of my movement, but the pain was still excruciating. I had improved enough to be able to run a distance of about 10 kilometres. I was afraid to push myself beyond what I had already done in the fear that it would take me back to being fully paralysed again. The positive side effect of my efforts had been the steady build-up of my stamina.

It was at this time that I got an opportunity to go diving, a sport that I had always enjoyed. My concern was the weight of the oxygen cylinder on my back. After some deliberation, I chose to discuss it with my doctor. While he had suggested pushing my boundaries, he hadn't expected me to take it this far. His immediate reaction was 'definitely not'. But I persisted and he agreed reluctantly.

I went diving and enjoyed every bit of it, marvelling at the fact that eighteen months back, I would not have believed that I would be back under 50 feet of water. Life looked beautiful. While the pain that followed lasted over a week, I still believe to this day that it was a good decision to dive again.

With that goal achieved, what next? A half marathon? What is life if you are always a conformist? Calculated risks have been the theme of my life, and I continued pushing even further. The eighteen months had made me addicted to being active. If I did not exert myself, I got extremely irritable and found inactivity terribly tiresome. Even today, it has become the answer to laziness and maintaining a positive attitude.

My confidence surged as I learnt to manage the pain. I decided that it was time to live up to the promise I made to myself. While I knew it would be extremely difficult, I started to believe that the attitude and confidence that I had developed would carry me through the trek to the EBC.

THREE

THE GOAL

AS AN AMATEUR, the first step in my journey was to spend time on research. While the amount of information available is enormous, I was unable to find a single source for basic guidelines on what I should or should not do. How severe would the climb be? Could I handle it with my back being in the condition it was? How best could I minimize the pain on the trek? Along with research, I spoke to several people who had a lot of experience trekking in the Himalayas.

As is the case with any project, planning is as important as its execution. This trip was no different. As this was my first trek, I was trying hard not to be too ambitious. I was a novice, totally inexperienced, and I didn't know what to expect. All I had was a goal and a dream. My research revealed that regular GPS/maps don't work or are untrustworthy; therefore, getting a reliable guide assumed paramount importance. Given the condition of my back, I wanted to make sure that I gave myself ample time for acclimatization, managing the pain and uncertainties that came with it. This potentially meant shorter trekking days with a time for rest each day. I realized that I should not 'try to conquer' all the mountains on my first trek, one of the best philosophies I adopted. Tremendous work and research resulted in a semi-optimized itinerary that ensured adequate time and stayed within my budget, including contingencies that might (and did) arise. Having the right gear and clothing was critical, as temperatures could drop to -25 degrees Centigrade in the mountains. As someone who likes to err on the side of caution, I made copious notes and plans to make sure I had much more than what I expected to need.

Once I had the plan, the logistics at home and the office had to be sorted out. The extended period of absence had to be accounted for and compensated for. With a firm plan, a date, and immense confidence, I went to see my orthopaedic surgeon five months before the tentative date of the trip. A tiny voice in me was nervous that he might say 'no'.

As soon as I entered his consulting room, I introduced the topic of trekking up to the EBC. It was a fairly short discussion, and a few minutes proved my fears

NO. DON'T EVEN THINK ABOUT IT. IT WILL BE TOO MUCH. IF YOU GO, I AM SURE TO SEE YOU ON THE SURGERY TABLE. IT DAWNED ON ME THAT I WAS BLESSED WITH A FANTASTIC FAMILY AND WONDERFUL FRIENDS. THERE ARE ONLY TWO KINDS OF PEOPLE IN ANY SITUATION, WINNERS AND LOSERS. THERE IS NO SECOND PLACE.

right. He said, 'No. Don't even think about it. It will be too much. If you go, I am sure to see you on the surgery table.'

I told him about the promise I had made to myself lying on that bed in the Emergency room. I tried in vain to explain why it was critical that I keep the promise. I was not willing to accept 'no' for an answer. Just as my teenage daughter does with me, I started 'negotiating' with the doctor.

Whether it was because he understood my mental predicament or he just did not want to listen to me any more, we reached the mutually amicable conclusion

that we would not decide at that point but would 'discuss' the issue three weeks before the actual trip and then take a final decision.

At least that is what my determined one-track mind heard and processed. My doctor had tried to avoid an argument with me but the fact that he didn't forbid me outright gave me hope. To me, 'Let's talk three weeks before the trip' translated to 'Get ready to go.' With this 'semi-okay' from the doctor, I returned home, excited.

On my drive back to my house, I wondered what the reaction of my family would be. I had been talking to my family about this throughout the period of my recovery and they had never objected to it, either because they did not believe it would ever happen or were truly supportive of my goals.

That evening, I had a detailed discussion with my family and a few close friends. It dawned on me that I was blessed with a fantastic family and wonderful friends. Every single one of them were extremely concerned, but were genuinely supportive because they knew it would mean a lot to me.

Goals motivate me. If I have a goal I am committed to, I almost always function better. I believe that if a person works really hard and, most importantly, is committed to a goal, nothing can stop him or her. The other factor that drives me is peer pressure. My personality is such that I need to win. I hate losing. I have always held the view that there are only two kinds of people in any situation, winners and losers. There is no second place.

Passion is a word that means more than one can imagine. Nothing worthwhile in the world has ever been achieved without it. I was passionate about making it to the top, and I was committed.

I knew a journey such as this is never done alone and always needs a good team. So I spent the next month on recruiting friends. This turned out to be much harder than I expected. There were too many requirements that had to be satisfied, beginning with the fact that the friends I chose had to be as passionate about trekking and climbing as I was. They had to be willing to take the required time off and to spend the money that was needed. Most importantly, I needed a team with whom I would be willing to spend every moment of fifteen to twenty days of my life.

This last condition was indeed a big hurdle to overcome. The colleagues I was indifferent to were the first to be struck off the list. And even the friends I hung out with had to be carefully evaluated—this was a matter of 24 x 7 x 15, a lot of time without a break.

I also had to sift through many other criteria such as my friends' commitments at work and at home; their health, their physical condition, and their mental fitness.

A number of discussions and conversations ensued. As can be expected, there were many yeses and semi-yeses, and outright nos. Over these conversations, I realised that I would not be able to get the friends I really wanted. So I quickly shifted gears to make sure that the people who agreed to come were people I could spend time with.

After several weeks of discussions and conversations, it came down to four people. While I did not know all them really well, I was very sure that I did not dislike them. Time would tell if I truly could afford to spend 24 x 7 x 15 with them.

FOUR

THE PREPARATION

THE TEAM OF FIVE WAS FINALISED—from 'I' it became 'We', and that was a wonderful feeling. All actions, thoughts, and conversations became much easier. In any group, the natural tendency is to feed off the emotions of one another, whether good or bad. We were no different.

Before I introduce the team members, it's only fair that I start with myself. I am Hari. No, it's not 'Harry', but 'Hari', close to 'hurry'. I was born into an average middle-class Indian family that always tried to do the right thing. It was a family that taught concepts such as, 'there is no substitute for hard work' or 'prayers work miracles'. High on emotions all the time, I often experience ups and downs. The classic feeling that I had not yet achieved a lot in my life was part of my mindset (and still is). Until a couple of years ago, I was on top of the world, but then my sudden paralysis and subsequent rehab brought some much-needed sanity in the sense that I realized there was something more to life than the everyday rat race.

Anamika is the member of our team I would like to first introduce. At the time we set out on the trek to the Everest, he was thirty-three years old, his receding hairline the bane of his existence. Nicknamed Anamika, which means being 'nameless', he had grown up in the shadow of an extremely successful father and sister (and a beautiful mother who supported them), and the thought that he had to accomplish much more in life weighed heavily on his mind. He believed he was smart, but took pride in the fact that this made others believe they were smarter. His smile always reflected his 'the-glass-is-half-full' and 'life is awesome' attitude. He had spent his childhood and youth in cities around the world, which made him extremely quick-witted; he usually has his audiences cracking up in no time. Even before we began planning our trip in earnest, he would ask me question after question about what lay ahead quite relentlessly.

Pappu, again a nickname, was a man who believed in careful planning. An introvert, he was usually careful to gauge his audience before he spoke. He was generally curious about almost everything, and was a far better listener than a speaker. As a responsible father and husband, he had spent the better part of his life doing what's right. A good student in school, he had studied at excellent universities and graduated summa cum laude. His hard work and sincerity continued as he joined the workforce, and he made fairly quick and healthy strides up the corporate ladder. Middle age caught up quickly, and he realized that life was zipping by—which is why this trip offered him the opportunity for him to do something new, something different. His physical appearance gave the impression that he could not make it past a kilometre on his best day. In the pursuit of his personal and professional goals, the trip to the gym had long been forgotten. However, over the few months of our preparation, he had been the most disciplined in exercising, meticulous in burning those calories and gaining stamina.

The next member I want to introduce is 'Lifebuoy', his nickname derived from the soap of the same name. It did not take a lot to make him smile. He was the happiest person in the world if he was acknowledged as the 'He Man' of the group. It was as if he'd come straight out of the Village People's (American disco group) song 'Macho Man'. Tall and well-built, his biggest pride was his well-sculpted body. Later, on

our arduous trek in the mountains, he'd say, 'It's only -20 degrees Centigrade, I don't need a sweater,' and shiver if it meant he would be acknowledged as the man of strength. He was strong and always had the 'Big brother is protecting you, so don't worry' aura about him. In the context of the Hindu religion, he would be closest to the monkey god Hanuman for his strength and fitness.

I REALIZED THERE WAS SOMETHING MORE TO LIFE THAN THE EVERYDAY RAT RACE.

He had grown up in the city of Kolkata in the state of West Bengal, and was the perfect symbol of the old value systems blending into the modern world. A member of a tightly knit family, he had lost his dad, his idol, a few months earlier. His value system kept him extremely honest and straightforward, not always a good combination in the corporate world, or the hospitality industry, where he had worked for most of his career.

The last member of our team to come down was 'MM'. He was born in Hyderabad, India, and was brought up there. He came from a traditional middle-class family, and worked hard to keep his grades up and his parents happy. At one point in his career, having climbed up the corporate ladder, he decided to work in the US. After over a decade, when he could no longer ignore the call of his home country, he headed back to India. It was then that his parents found him a wife and he soon became the father of two wonderful children. He was smart, very analytical, and very curious. He needed to know everything about everything, and wouldn't be comfortable 'winging' it. He needed the clarity of black and white, with minimal or no grey at all.

Physically, he was of average height and build. He was middle-aged, and suffered from the 'I have not done anything yet in my life' syndrome that all of us go through. He was excitable, but could get low-spirited equally quickly.

The anticipation built up to a crescendo over the next two months; the trip took centre-stage at all gatherings, whether among the team itself or with friends or acquaintances, some of whom were detached, some envious, while others wanted to be a part of the conversation. It was a whole lot of fun talking, chatting and discussing our plans. As I look back, those were some of the best memories of the trip.

It was in the afternoon of one of those days when I had a relapse and the back pain returned. It had been

two years of learning to manage the pain and building confidence, but that afternoon, I felt mentally weak. The pain was radiating all through my body.

Two years of suffering had taught me that one of the best courses of action is to lie flat on a really hard surface (like the floor) and do nothing. I could not read, or watch TV, or move my neck. It was very difficult, since all I could do—and did—was stare at the ceiling. But I had no choice. Going offline cold turkey became therapy in itself. It provided the perfect break from the daily routine to pause, reflect, and relax.

As I lay there staring at the ceiling, I wondered why the stress levels had shot up. Was it the pressure that I was facing at work trying to wrap up before I left or was it the possibility that my body would be completely paralysed? As I thought hard and deeply, I suddenly realized that it might just be the fear of failure. What if I failed in my quest and had to come back to face my family and friends? Was this the classic, 'what if I fail?' scenario that we experience in our daily lives? As I worked hard to slow down my racing heart and mind, I grew concerned. What if this happened during the trip? How would I manage? As I lay there, I knew I would have to wrestle with many such thoughts throughout the journey and would have to find it within myself each time to push past the pain and remember the goal.

I forced myself to think positively. How wonderful it would be if I completed the trip successfully! As the pain subsided in my back, I wondered why I was so excited about this whole trip? Why was there this general sense of heightened excitement accompanied by the fear that I might not be able to go through it? I think it was the thrill of going on an adventure and overcoming obstacles, since mountain climbing was new to me.

Hearing that I had a bad spell and was laid up, a friend of mine came over with dinner for me. The medications and a few hours of rest had lowered the pain by a few degrees. I propped myself on a pillow and felt much better after a little food in my belly.

After my friend left, I lay back thinking. I had a good lifestyle and a job that paid really well; I had a home, a family, and wonderful friends. But I was still very much a part of the corporate rat race. Why was it that what I had wasn't enough? Was it a desire for more wealth—which is highly unlike me—or because my peers earned more than I did? Was life about living by comparison? I wondered why we often look for the approval and validation of others even when we know we are happy and doing something well. Was this trek going to give me that elusive sense of accomplishment and satisfaction?

The evening turned to night. The pain that had lessened earlier had shot back up. I was certain this was more fear than physical pain. I decided that I had no choice but to argue myself out of my fears, take some more medicines, and go to bed that night. When I woke up the next day, the pain had dropped precipitously. I was not sure if the meds were working or I was less stressed. Psychologically, I felt a lot better as well. It was a relief that is tough to describe. I spent the next few days on the Internet gathering checklists, purchase lists, shopping lists ... For this trip, there were lists for almost everything, from the abstract to the material—Top Ten things to remember; Top Five things not to forget; Top Ten things to never do; Top Seven things to always keep handy; and so on.

As wonderful as the Internet is, I reconfirmed through this process that it is the largest garbage dump of data in the world. Distilling information was a serious challenge. Confirming that the information was reliable was even tougher. Fortunately for me, many of my friends as well as my wife had done some of these trips before, and they helped me filter the lists down. They helped me pare them down and make them more practical and realistic. I decided to rely on them a lot more than the data available online.

It is often said that it's the journey that's important, and not necessarily the destination. As a goal-oriented person, this has not been strictly true for me, and this was a destination that was important for me to reach. But I constantly reminded myself to enjoy every step of the way.

Given the gruelling nature of the trip and the fact that all five of us were rookies, the preparation was important and could not be trivialized. It was even more important for me, given my recent bout of back pain. We had to make sure that we packed items we would need daily, others that we would need some time during the trip, and those we might need under special circumstances or for emergencies.

We had multiple and animated discussions and deliberations on what to buy—equipment, food, clothes, and so on. Quality could not be compromised, especially for our equipment. Safety was obviously non-negotiable, and comfort was desirable.

As more and more people found out about our trip, a flood of questions was directed at us. Before we realized it, we had become masters of the fine art of exaggeration, making the trip seem a lot more arduous, strenuous, and most definitely ominous. We were caught in the vicious cycle of trying to outdo ourselves as we answered questions—I attribute this to our growing excitement and very patient, yet gullible listeners. The art of embellishment was definitely pushed to the limit by us, investing the trip with the glamour of a mission to the moon or into space. But every time we spun a story, our egos got a boost and raised the excitement levels sky high.

FIVE

GETTING FIT

THE ENTHUSIASM CONTINUED TO GROW and became contagious. There were days when it felt like we were high on some prohibited substance. But we knew this fever-pitch of excitement would crash and burn in the harsh conditions of the mountains if we weren't prepared for it physically. We definitely weren't going to fail because of that, and decided to get our bodies into shape.

To be honest, we were definitely not in the best shape physically. Once again, after sifting through endless data online, we decided on exercises that built stamina and on breathing techniques that would help as at high altitudes. We made a firm pact to ourselves to be extremely disciplined and hit the gym regularly. We were short on time, but a long way to go in whipping our bodies into shape.

Within a couple of weeks, we realized that these goals had become like 'New Year resolutions' that don't last past the first two weeks of January. Between the inherent inertia and our professional and personal schedules, finding time for training became difficult. But we had to take measures to make it to the Everest Base Camp without embarrassing ourselves.

Fear of failure can be an extremely strong motivator. I did not want to even entertain the thought of not reaching the top—I wasn't sure my ego would recover if we did not reach it after all the talk and excitement. I wonder how often a negative thought (such as fear of failure) drives one to positive behaviour or gives one enough determination to push forward. I'm not sure of the answer, but in my case, it certainly seems to be more often than not.

Given the condition of my back and the persistent pain, my anxiety levels were high. The growing expectations—my own and those of my peers—were taking their toll on me. Added to this was my stubborn Type-A personality—I cannot and will not fail. I began to push myself pretty hard. I needed to exercise; I needed to feel confident that my back would hold and that I would not fail. I needed to make a routine out of exercising. Whether it was walking, trekking, running, or swimming I wanted to exercise at least three to four times a week so that I could comfortably cover a distance of at least 10 kilometres on inclines.

However, my work schedule was extremely hectic and unrelenting. At that time, I was travelling for about three weeks in a month, between continents. Regardless of the comforts of first-class travel, it was physically and mentally exhausting. I was at a stage where it took me over eight days to recover from each trip. But almost before I could recover, I was back on the road again. This constant travel, combined with the heavy workload, and the big factor of constant jet lag was playing havoc with my body clock. I struggled to find even an hour each day to exercise. And each day that I did not exercise, I tried to convince myself that my problems were real and that I was not just trying to come up with excuses.

Whenever my guilt managed to overcome my excuses, I miraculously found the time and energy to exercise. I began to wonder if this was another mental block and not a physical or logistical one. I did push against the inertia to go out to exercise a few times. When the weather was not conducive for outdoor exercise, I would get on a stationary bike in the gym.

Adding to this annoyance was my infamous stomach: I have been diagnosed with Irritable Bowel Syndrome or IBS. It seemed that almost all my problems seem to affect my stomach. I'm not sure what sets it off, because anything, from physical or mental stress, to all sorts of food—rice, wheat, fruit, vegetables, meat—can trigger it at any time. The resulting upset stomach weakens me physically to the point where I have to lie down. This makes me even more tense and so prolongs the upset stomach condition in a vicious cycle.

FEAR OF FAILURE CAN BE AN EXTREMELY STRONG MOTIVATOR

I was currently going through one such cycle. I kept telling myself to relax, that this bout was no different than most days in the last ten years. But what worried me was that it could also happen during the trip.

Despite all this, neither my workload nor the travel showed any signs of letting up. Rather, it increased even more because I had to ensure that the office ran smoothly when I was away. The extra work this required caused serious problems with my exercise routine, and at one point, almost stamped it out.

However, I managed to get some training in. On some days, I was even able to run or trek about 10 kilometres.

Going off the usual route and discovering new and different areas of my neighbourhood helped break the monotony and motivated me to try even harder.

SIX

THE FINAL DAYS BEFORE THE TRIP

SINCE TREKKING SHOES WAS ONE of the most critical pieces of the equipment needed, I bought myself a sturdy pair from REI. The unusually cold winter in the US gave me the perfect opportunity to try them on through snow, ice, and slush, which I would encounter on the trip as well. They were excellent shoes, but over time I realized that they had very stiff soles that would begin to hurt after a while. So I went back a few days later to exchange them for a better pair. The new brand that I bought this time had softer soles, were comfortable, waterproof and kept my feet warm.

The five of us continued to talk about and deliberate about what we should carry with us. Our guide had told us on the phone that the total amount of luggage per person (including food, clothing, and equipment) could not exceed 15 kilograms. This required drastic elimination of items after we relied quite heavily on advice from friends and family who had actual climbing experience.

I LAY AWAKE IN BED MANY NIGHTS WONDERING, 'CAN I MAKE IT?'

As the days progressed, the enormity of the expedition became a reality. I am not sure if it was the excitement, the nervousness, or equal measures of both that prompted us to plan big, but the blend of enthusiasm and fear was definitely palpable. Some discussions revolved on how to best document our achievement. I decided that I would keep daily journals, written and video-taped, to capture significant moments of the journey. I got myself a really good HD video camera that weighed almost nothing and several batteries that could last for days and memory cards. I wasn't leaving anything to chance. As trivial as it sounds, we had some serious deliberations on how often I was going to record my video journal—whether every day or on alternate days, or only to capture the highlights and milestones. A part of me wondered why we were discussing camera options when the really serious issues of stamina, health, risks and hazards were still looming large.

Even as the excitement and anxiety built up, I lay awake in bed many nights wondering, 'Can I make it? Is it possible?' Behind all the hype, the fear of failure was getting more intense.

SEVEN

THE DAY BEFORE THE TRIP

AT LAST CAME THE DAY before we were to leave. Lists, purchases, exercise regimens, were all a thing of the past. The five of us were so excited that we were not thinking clearly when we met in my apartment that morning to decide the final logistics. We had to decide who would carry what within the limited weight restriction of 15 kilograms. As this included all clothing, food, equipment, sleeping bags and other items, 15 kilograms seemed too little. Hence we struggled between caution and exceeding the weight restrictions. It was one of our first lessons in teamwork and learning to depend on one another. It did not matter what each of us carried—what mattered was that together we would manage to take all we would need for the entire trip.

Our adrenaline levels were sky-high. We spoke in circles and pentagons and hexagons—never getting to any point. Too much excitement turns people crazy, and that is precisely what was happening. No productive decisions were made for 105 minutes. I looked at the watch and told the team that in fifteen minutes, the married two would face the curfew imposed by their spouses. So what we did not do in 105 minutes of deliberations got sorted out in the next fifteen—our luggage issues, shopping lists, assigning responsibilities, deciding on the clothes to take. Clothing was crucial for we needed three 'levels'—the first level of winter clothing for up to 5000 feet (1500 metres); the next level of winter clothing, such as lined jackets, gloves, and thermals, for lower temperatures and wind chills at 10,000 feet (3000 metres); the third level was bulky stuff for heights beyond 10,000 feet, such as down jackets, multiple layers of gloves, multiple 'smartwool' socks, chemical warmers, UV protection, grade four sunglasses, and multiple thick thermals.

I'M NOT GOING TO LET ANYTHING STOP ME.

Before we parted for the day, I whipped out the new video camera. I decided to begin my video journal with capturing this moment when the team was together, happy and ready to take on the challenge. It was the first time I was reporting for the journal with the team on camera for the first time—we had a lot of fun behaving like idiots, enjoying each anticipatory moment.

After everyone left and things had quieted down, I sat down to do a final inventory and cross-referenced it against the lists we had just agreed upon—a sort of 'what I have and what is missing' list. I concentrated on thinking through what I would need each day of the trip as best as I could. While it was standard travel planning, I had to focus on what I needed for my medical condition with special care. I was not ready to fail for any reasons that were in my control.

'I'm not going to let anything stop me.' I kept telling myself this repeatedly to prepare my mind for the tough mental and physical challenges ahead. My introspection and then scrutiny of all the items laid out in front of me, calmed me down a bit. It was going to be a long day of getting through last-minute purchases and other logistical arrangements and I had to be in the right frame of mind.

For a moment, I pondered over my back problem again because I felt the pain returning. Nervousness combined with excitement is never a good formula for anybody. I strongly believe that stress is the biggest disease in the world, that other than physical

injuries, almost all illnesses are caused by stress. We have not even skimmed the surface when it comes to understanding the human body. Despite so much progress in the field of medical science, we don't have the faintest clue when it comes to defining what stress truly is. The sufferer does not even recognize it easily as its symptomatic manifestations are so varied.

My current situation was no different. The overall stress of the situation had manifested as a sore throat. Though I immediately started medications to fight it, I felt feverish. I was not feeling 100 per cent anymore, and being weak, I decided not to exercise. I reminded myself that it was the last day before the trip and there was not a lot I could do now. I would either have enough stamina to climb all the way to the EBC or not. Skipping exercise on this day was not going to make a difference.

I lay down for a couple of hours. The feverishness had not left me yet, but I was not going to let some ridiculous freakish infection defeat me. I forced myself out of bed and stepped out to get my last-minute shopping done. I downloaded a few books onto my Kindle so I could read during the evenings after a long day of trekking. I also rechecked that the batteries for my video camera were charged and tested it out by recording a video journal for the day before the trip.

The sun had set and the day had flown by without me even realizing it. I managed to gulp down some dinner, and after praying for physical and mental strength the following day, I decided to retire early. The alarm was kept for an early morning wake-up call and trying to curb the anxiety regarding an early morning trip to the airport, I slept.

EIGHT

DAY ONE
On a High

I WOKE UP BEFORE THE ALARM went off. The day I had been working towards had finally arrived! The back pain and the illness that I had been experiencing the last few days miraculously gave way to complete happiness and determination. I had a spring in my step that morning.

I was already in Hyderabad in India that morning after a flight from the US a couple of days back. After an easy twenty-five-minute cab ride, I reached the Hyderabad airport early and was checked in quickly. Our flight to Kathmandu was to be through Mumbai. I managed to get some breakfast at the airport and met the team. To our relief, the flight was on time, a good start to the day.

The flight landed in Mumbai incident-free. We had just spent close to three hours as a group, early times for five men who did not know each other too well and were trying to bond. So far, it was the honeymoon period, and things were looking good. When you smile and are happy, the world seems happy and smiles back at you. All five of us were high on life that day, so we took the standard Indian delays—'Bus will leave now' (and not leave for an hour) or 'It will be done in ten minutes' (and take over thirty)—all in our stride. In fact, we did not even think about all the delays and issues till much later. At the Mumbai airport, we had to transfer to the new international terminal as we were headed out of the country. When we got there and checked in, we were told we had to get back to the domestic terminal to board our flight as it was departing from there. The airport was being renovated and, needless to say, a complete logistical mess. But we were unfazed. After several back and forth transfers (lack of coordination amongst the airport officials adding to the confusion), we boarded our plane. It was a short two-hour flight to Kathmandu aboard an A320 aircraft.

TRAVEL HAS BEEN A PART OF MY LIFE FOR THE LAST EIGHTEEN YEARS. IN FACT IT HAS DEFINED IT

Travel has been a part of my life for the last eighteen years. In fact, it has defined it. I fly over 200,000 miles (320,000 kilometres) every year. That's a lot of frequent flier miles—I can give George Clooney's character from *Up in the Air* a run for his money. Though it is—and has been—difficult, travel has helped define my personality and has given me traits like patience. It has taught me things about life that no book or educational university can. It is said that, 'The world is a book and those who do not travel read only a page'—and I would say that those who don't travel don't live.

Our excitement continued unabated until we landed in Kathmandu. I am sure we came across as people who were travelling by plane for the first time. We were noisy, taking pictures and laughing at almost anything. I am sure we managed to annoy a lot of people on that plane. We were the same people that I hate on my planes. But we were so high on life at that point that we really did not care or pause to think about it. We soon landed in Kathmandu—a small, ancient city with an extremely messy international airport stuck in the procedures and infrastructure of the 1970s.

NINE

REALITY CHECK

THE KATHMANDU AIRPORT was a sorry excuse for an international airport. The infrastructure was abysmal and the processes and procedures antiquated. There were some (Indians) who were let through just based on an Indian driving licence (and no passport), and then there were others who had to fill out forms and pay a lot of money for the sticker that was the visa. There was hardly any signboards to guide passengers through what they had to do. It was pure guesswork and inquiries, and it took us a while to figure out what to do. It took us even longer to find the correct forms, then the correct place to queue up to get approval for entry.

Long queues and a determined exercise in patience later, we stepped out into the city of Kathmandu, the capital of Nepal. A warm and sunny day greeted us with temperatures hovering around 18 degrees Centigrade. Our guide, Tikka, was waiting outside. He and his group of Sherpas greeted us with traditional Nepalese hospitality, presenting us with garlands of flowers. A couple of us decided to spent some time trying to get local SIM cards for our cell phones, which later turned out to be a waste of time as they never worked in the mountains. We exchanged the usual pleasantries and then got into our transfer vehicle to get to the hotel. Tikka was very pleasant, and we managed to communicate despite his broken English. The desire to please one's guest, a trait that defines the Nepalese culture, was evident from the first greeting.

The city of Kathmandu seemed ragged and beaten down. Located in a beautiful valley, it's the only large urban city in Nepal with a population of over 3 million people and spread over about 50 square kilometres. Surrounded by mountains, it enjoys a temperate climate and appears lush green. Over the decade, Nepal has relied on tourism as its largest industry to sustain its economy.

Kathmandu, with an extremely rich history of over 2000 years, is caught in the throes of transforming into a modern city of concrete and steel. It is draped in old traditions and is now struggling to adopt the ways and means of the modern world. All the fundamental elements of a city like transportation, infrastructure and so on remain antiquated, giving the impression of a poor city. The architecture of the city is a blend of some of the finer elements from both Hinduism and Buddhism. Overall, it was extremely polluted, its permanent dust cover giving it a feel of dirtiness, and had a very weak infrastructure. The first impression I got was that time has stood still from mid-1970s: narrow roads, buildings that had seen better times decades ago, vehicles that desperately needed to be cleaned and upgraded, and even hospitals that needed a coat of paint at the very least. Traffic was down to a crawl, automobiles honking and music players blaring filled the air. The weather felt hot and humid though the temperature was about 18 degrees Centigrade.

WHY ARE WE IN THE RAT RACE? WHAT ARE WE TRYING TO ACHIEVE? TIME TO PAUSE AND 'SMELL THE ROSES'

Amidst the dirt and mess on the side of a road, I saw a small kid wearing ragged clothes playing with a single rubber tube from a bicycle. He had dirt and grime all over him, but absorbed in his game, the most beautiful smile adorned his face. He was happy, without a care in this world. I saw his mother come out, pick him up and plant a kiss on his face.

Life is a juxtaposition of feelings. While the sight of the small boy was not new to me, it made me realize that it is not the concrete of the city, the buildings or a new coat of paint that can give happiness; it is always found within. Kathmandu was no different.

After driving through what felt like most of the city, we reached our hotel, Shangri-La. The reception confirmed my impression that Kathmandu was a laidback city where not a lot moved until about 10 or 11 a.m. It was similar to many cities in the Indian subcontinent where the business day begins around 10 a.m. or later. In contrast with the rat race that begins around 6 a.m. in cities like New York, London, or Mumbai, the city of Kathmandu provided a respite. It was refreshing and begged the question—why are we in the rat race? What are we trying to achieve? We work hard all our lives to make sure we can enjoy our retirement, but when we get to that age, we just don't have the energy or capability to enjoy it. So what are we then truly after? It is wonderful to see a part of the world that still takes the time to pause and 'smell the roses'. It reminded me of the villages and some small cities in India where the shops open no earlier than 10.30 a.m. By 1 p.m. they are shut and people go home, lunch and take an afternoon nap and return to work at around 4 p.m., a relaxed, peaceful way of life.

As I reflected on this, I realized that almost all the cities in the so-called 'developed' countries are crazily in the rat race. So are they truly 'developed'? If so, in what sense? Developed in the craziness of the rat race? The intensity in the focus of 'killing' themselves and not having a 'true' life? Or in talking about 'flexibility' and calling themselves 'advanced'? 'Developed' countries are said to have a high standard of living compared to the 'developing' countries, but I wondered what we'd say if we measured happiness instead? Kathmandu made me reflect on what happiness truly means.

As the day progressed, our energy levels began to dip. I still felt physically weak, but better. I wondered if it was the fall after the earlier adrenaline rush? Or was it simply the fact that I was in a happy state of mind? Either way, I felt like I was ready to conquer the world.

TEN

LUNCH AND A LATE INTRODUCTION

AFTER WE SETTLED DOWN in our rooms at the hotel, we decided to meet for a really late lunch. I was the first to arrive at the hotel's restaurant. I found myself a seat in a corner and was soon lost in thought. We were a diverse bunch of people, whose personalities were slowly being revealed. I realized that there would be plenty of time to get to know the team members better over the next couple of weeks. From the little that I had seen of them, two were spontaneous and easy-going, while the other two seemed serious and needed to lighten up and have some fun. I was hoping this trip would be the best place for them to do so.

Now that we were all present, we needed to iron out a lot of the finer details of the next two weeks. We had to sort out some of the finances for the trip with the guides and organizers. We also needed to have a frank chat with them about what we needed to do, what to expect on the trip, and so on—all natural questions that one could expect from amateurs on their first trip.

Tikka, our main guide, was not the most fluent in the English language and this meant that we needed to have patience as we listened to the details and instructions. As the 'big picture' guy, I always have complete confidence that people will handle a situation to the best of their abilities. This means that micromanaging is not a word in my professional dictionary. So I tried to shape Tikka's instructions and suggestions into a plan we could execute as a team.

The conversation centred on our plans for the next few days. Tikka and the trip organizer informed us that in addition himself, we were going to need a Sherpa and three porters to carry our bags. Ming Ma was introduced to us as the Sherpa who would be joining us.

MM's focused attention to detail came in handy as he and Anamika worked out the financial agenda. Ming Ma gave us five bags, one for each of us to pack all the things we would need for the next two weeks—clothes, equipment, liners, food, snacks and other items. Even though we had carefully planned the 15 kilograms we needed to take, we still had to—literally—weigh our options once again. In the end, we decided to wear our heavy trekking shoes instead of packing them, hoping to lighten the bags by at least 2 kilograms each.

WHY DO YOU HAVE 15 KILOGRAMS AS A LIMIT? WE DECIDED TO BE SMART ABOUT IT AND CATEGORIZED ALL WE HAD INTO THE 'MUST HAVES', 'WOULD LIKE TO HAVES', AND THE 'NICE TO HAVES'

Hooray—we did it! We had managed to squeeze stuff into our individual bags without them weighing even a fraction more than 15 kilograms, but our delight was short-lived. Before we were done congratulating ourselves for this 'achievement', Tikka came with down jackets for higher altitudes, liners, and sleeping bags and told us that we needed to carry those as well.

We looked at each other nervously, concluding that this was an impossible task, and were general cursing the situation until MM decided to ask a simple question, 'Why do you have 15 kilograms as a limit?.' Tikka responded that each porter would carry two of these bags on their shoulders when they climbed up with us, hinting that it was humane to lighten their burden. It was a rude awakening for me as I had never paused to think about the porters' burdens. I was determined to restrict the weight to as little as I could.

Lunch arrived in the middle of our discussion and we suddenly realized we were really hungry. It was almost 4 p.m. and we had not eaten since breakfast—and so the food tasted quite good.

We decided that we could not pack anymore at that point and deferred the rest of the task of packing to the night. We planned to go shopping the next day to buy our last-minute gear and clothing at Thamel, a small suburb of Kathmandu. Thamel has become popular with adventure and outdoor enthusiasts for its knock-offs on equipment, clothing and other items required for hiking, trekking, climbing. Cheap Chinese products flood the shops with no respect for patents or copyrights. As much as I hate the lack of control in intellectual property protection, like any normal human being, I am attracted to cheap prices and we found the counterfeit goods were available at very reasonable prices.

Over the last two months, I had insisted on purchasing most of the required items from Thamel, as many friends had told me that I could get a lot of clothing (from several brands such as Northface, Reebok) in Thamel at really cheap prices. My constant 'sales pitch' earned me the title of 'The Merchant of Thamel'.

We had an early start the next day, but since we did not have adequate clothes, such as pants, dry-fits and so on, we had no choice but to buy whatever we could find in the stores in Thamel before they closed down for the day. So with a 'gun to our head', we began rushing between stores to find what we needed. It was then that we came across the 'Nasha Bar'. We were five guys in a state of 'nasha' or 'intoxication', who had just come across a strip club in a foreign city. In spite of the fact that we were in a hurry, the catchy name and our state of mind made us pause outside for a moment. Though we quickly concluded that we did not have time to go to the bar that night, we promised to reward ourselves with a visit there after our trek. Anamika and I were in our element, talking about topics triggered by Nasha Bar. While Lifebuoy got into the conversation slowly, MM, who I thought was the most excited—and bursting at the seams to speak—kept quiet. It was still early days for our team, and I guessed he was not yet ready to talk about sex. The chats continued as we walked between the shops at Thamel. As in a typical local market, haggling was the order of the day and we got good deals.

After a quick shower back in the hotel, we hurried to a dinner arranged by the Indian Attaché to Nepal. Anamika's father, a high-ranking official in the Indian government was excited about his son's adventure had contacted the Indian Attaché to Nepal, who invited us. Although we were neither hungry nor keen on going, we could not find a way to get out of the commitment so went begrudgingly. The irony was that we enjoyed the evening a lot—and before we knew it, time had flown by and we were really late getting back.

The plan had been to leave before the crack of dawn the next day so that we could catch our flight to Lukla, a town near the Everest, which meant that we had to pack immediately. We got busy. The 15-kilogram limit kept haunting us. How were we supposed to fit all the stuff we needed into a single duffel bag? We sorted and prioritized—and then did it again, but it would not fit. We packed, repacked, and tried every technique we could, but each bag was simply not large enough to accommodate everything. We were nervous because we did not know what to choose. For all we knew, Murphy's law would factor in and we would need the one item that we left behind.

We decided to be smart about it and categorized all we had into the 'must haves', 'would like to haves', and the 'nice to haves'. A few hard decisions later, we were down to a single duffel bag each. We hit the bed, realizing that we had to wake up in less than five hours. The exhaustion from the day's activities and the lack of sleep from the previous night got the better of me, and I slept peacefully.

ELEVEN

DAY TWO
Off to the Mountains

MY DEEP SLEEP WAS DISRUPTED by the alarm going off. I usually wake up before the alarm so I woke up with a start. Though still sleepy, the excitement got us to our feet pretty quickly. As we went about scrambling through the morning chores, Sherpa Ming Ma came to pick up the luggage. This was it! We were all set and ready to start out on the first day of our trip.

Given the time constraints, we did not have even a moment to have breakfast. Realizing this, Tikka had breakfast packets waiting for us in the transfer van. Luggage was loaded onto the van and we were headed for the Kathmandu domestic airport to catch our flight to Lukla.

The traffic was light in the early hours of the day, and we reached the airport in good time. The airport looked like a chaotic bus stand, bustling with people, and it was far too noisy. Inside wasn't much better—it was a single large hall with a few small rooms that served as offices. It was a complete mess, in shambles and stinking. Chaotic all around, there was no organization or discipline and the security set-up was non-existent or rudimentary at best.

I was glad that we had Tikka with us. I wasn't sure we'd have been able to check-in or find a flight otherwise. Tikka asked us to wait and went to find out about our flight to Lukla. About twenty minutes later, he came back to tell us that we had been taken off our original flight and had to wait for the next one. This got me curious—we had reached the airport well on time, our flight was on time as well, and as laid down by the Geneva and Warsaw conventions that govern air traffic across the world, no airline could bump us off without our authorization and adequate compensation. I had to investigate.

I asked Tikka and a couple of other locals who could speak either English or Hindi, and after a serious inquisition, I learnt that domestic flights in the Kathmandu airport did not follow any rules. They were literally like local city buses with scant regard for reservations—a passenger buys a ticket for a destination and boards the next available flight for there are no formal confirmations other than the fact that a ticket was booked. No seats or flight numbers are assigned. The boarding pass was also very similar to a bus ticket. This was definitely a surprise for me and I wondered if this caused major security concerns. But that was the system, and the only choice we had was to fit right into it. Unfortunately, this meant a wait of more than an hour. As the infrastructure was abysmal, even the basic amenities of food and toilets were either absent or inadequate.

The delay of an hour stretched to two hours. Since I was still in an excited state of mind, I decided to take it in my stride. As I pondered over the happenings of the last forty-eight hours, I continued to feel a little anxious about whether I could succeed. Waiting for the flight, it was sinking in that the trip was actually happening. The dream was becoming a reality. It felt like the moments before a school exam. Although I'd been a good student and 'a teacher's pet' with strong confidence, I always got butterflies in my stomach before a test. I strongly believe that, like any other emotion, nervousness in moderation can help to achieve a positive outcome and on that day, I think I had the right amount to strengthen my determination.

As we five waited, we had time to chat and realized conversation was a little easier—we were beginning to appreciate enjoy each other's company more, and were more open with each other. At last, Tikka asked us to go through the security check, which turned out to be cursory at best, just a formality. Luckily, the holding area where we had to wait to board the flight was clean, orderly, had plenty of seating space for passengers and shops that sold snacks.

Another half an hour later, a bus took us to the aircraft, which we were told was a Dornier Do 228, with seating for sixteen passengers. To get the best view, we were advised to sit on the left—we were flying east, so the mountains would be on the left. To accomplish this, we had to be the first to board the flight. So we got on the bus early. The bus ride was long—and then the strangest thing happened, a first for me in all my travels—the aircraft hadn't yet arrived! When it finally did after about half and hour, we had to wait twenty minutes more for the plane to be refuelled and cleaned.

As soon as we'd boarded the plane and the doors were closed, we taxied out and finally, we were in the air! Within minutes, the entire scenery changed dramatically. The magnificence of the sight that greeted us was awe-inspiring. The hustle and bustle of the city gave way to one of the most stunning views I have seen in the world. We were literally on top of the world, cruising just above the tallest mountains, traversing right between them over the valleys. Sometimes words are difficult to describe an emotion such as the one I was experiencing. You need to be on that plane flying over those mountains to experience what I am trying— and failing—to describe. 'Imposing', 'majestic', and 'breathtaking', all describe the view inadequately.

Before we knew it, we were preparing to land. And just like that, my calm disappeared—for we were going to land in what National Geographic and the History Channel have categorized as the most dangerous airport in the world. I had seen the airport on YouTube several times before, but was still unnerved. Located at an elevation of 9,300 feet (2,860 metres) and rightfully named after the first people who conquered Mount Everest, the Tenzing–Hillary Airport is dangerous because of several factors:

1. The runway is only 1500 feet (460 metres) long and 65 feet (20 metres) wide (compare this to Chicago's, which is 13,000 feet (3,960 metres) long and 150 feet (46 metres) wide).

2. There is just one runway for landing (runway 06) and one for take-off (runway 24).

3. The landing is a sharp right turn from the valley into the runway.

4. The runway drops precipitously down a cliff at its end. So it can be fatal if you hit it early while landing or do not take off in time.

5. The runway is at a 12 degree incline, so the aircraft lands on top of the incline and takes off down it.

6. The weather can change dramatically in a very short time.

7. The landing depends on manual telemetry and judgement with the limited instruments on the Dornier. Thus, the margin for human error is huge.

As a private pilot who has flown smaller aircrafts, it was a totally exhilarating experience for me. I was in the first seat and watching the pilots (there was no door to the small cockpit) and the runway. Our pilots landed the aircraft as smoothly as possible and pulled into the small area that was used for deplaning and boarding. The small facade of the airport building made for a quick exit.

We walked around the airport building to the end of the runway perched on a hill and spent some time watching the aircrafts land and take off. I held my breath each time an aircraft rolled down the runway to take off. What if it did not muster enough speed and fell off the cliff? I could have continued to watch in awe for many more hours, but we had to proceed. We walked over to the local teahouse.

As we sat on the verandah of the teahouse, I was feeling a mystical high. I was dressed warmly in my jacket, protected from the cold air blowing through the valley. I was truly sitting in the lap of nature, surrounded by tall mountains and lush greenery, with snow visible at higher altitudes. The eerie silence that enveloped the valley was broken only by the sound of planes landing and taking off.

The porters brought our bags over, and then it was decision time. We needed to pull out the things we needed for that day's trek and transfer them to our own backpacks. Given it was the first day of our trek, I was not even sure what we would need. We were told that the porters would carry on ahead with the rest of the luggage to set up camp and meet us there when we caught up.

In spite of all our preparations and shopping, each of us had missed out some items like hats and sunglasses. So we had no choice but to stop at a small shop and buy them.

Our spirits were high as we set off, and we started clicking away to capture all the 'Kodak moments'. We paused many times to soak in the beauty of the mountains. They were of different kinds—small, majestic, barren, flat, or snow-clad, all beautiful beyond description. In the process, we slowed our progress down. But since the first day's trek was expected to be short, our schedule was okay. Naturally, as in the beginning of any adventure, the energy levels and enthusiasm were high. I pulled out my video camera to continue my video journal as we moved along, wondering how long this enthusiasm would last, and whether I was disciplined and committed enough to carry on till the end. I also thought of how to make my account for each day interesting for my audience. Although I had been a public speaker and could handle really large audiences, I was still very nervous in front of the camera.

The trek from Lukla began as a steep downhill descent into the valley of Chaurikharka. The trek was a breeze, although rocky for the most part, as we were full of energy and the effort required was minimal. As we made the first major turn on the trail, we were treated to some breathtaking out-of-the-world views of the mountains. This got us even more excited, if that was even possible, and many photographs, poses, and exclamations later, we carried on.

The entire trail was dotted intermittently with small villages. For the most part, the locals depended on tourists and trekkers for their income. The kids were adorable, but mostly shy—they'd been told to stay away from trekkers as a natural precaution. Some were extroverts and proactively tried to start a conversation with us in the local language, Nepalese. Since we did not know the language, it was a fun conversation, mostly unintelligible!

The morning trek was fascinating. As amateurs, we were discovering the fundamentals and were getting schooled quickly in trekking in the mountains. Once we hit the valley, the trail started to ascend, and our pace slowed down. The steeper it got, the more our energy waned, almost as if it was inversely proportionate to the incline. After a couple of hours and a few breaks for brief rests, we stopped at the hamlet of Cheplung 8700 feet (2660 metres) for lunch. This was the first teahouse of many that we would visit.

The Everest Base Camp trail is one of the most popular trails in the Himalayas, so the trekker traffic is quite dense. To cater to the tourists, plenty of teahouses dot the trail. To me, most of the them looked the same. Each teahouse was made of plywood and had a fairly big room with a coal or wood-fired boiler in the centre and a few tables and benches around it. The boiler was used to heat the room when it got really cold. Next to this room was the kitchen. Some of the larger teahouses offered accommodation too, small rooms with two bunks each.

It was when we sat down and placed our orders—soup, rice, and noodles—that we realized how exhausted we were. The anticipation and enthusiasm of the morning was wearing off and the ascent taking its toll. Still, we were slowly getting the hang of trekking and climbing.

I had been carrying my backpack all morning. The moment the weight of the bag was off, my muscles reacted and pain shot up through my body. I was writhing in pain. I felt helpless and without hope. Desperation swept through me and all my fears compounded were flashing in front of me. I was angry at myself. How could I have forgotten the basics of pain management? I had reminded myself to be careful every single day as I was preparing for this trip and in all the excitement of the first day, I had forgotten to do so. I could not bear the pain any longer, and warm tears started flowing down my cheeks. I turned away from the team and prayed for a miracle.

I couldn't have my regular painkillers because the blood dilator we'd been prescribed for altitude sickness wasn't compatible with them. And neither was it compatible with any medication in the ibuprofen, aceclofenac family, or, for that matter, with any muscle relaxant. I knew that if I did not take a painkiller, I wouldn't stand a chance of moving ahead. So, since the doctor had not expressly 'forbidden', but had 'recommended' that I not have the two together, I decided that it was worth the risk. I popped a couple of pills and lay down on one of the benches to keep my back straight.

In spite of the noise around, the medications, the pain, and the fatigue knocked me out, and soon I was half drifting off to sleep. I could hear the team talking quite loudly. Lifebuoy was excited and definitely wanted to be the macho man, explaining how he wasn't the slightest bit tired, so didn't need the offered trekking

THE DREAM WAS BECOMING A REALITY 'IMPOSING', 'MAJESTIC' 'BREATH-TAKING', ALL DESCRIBE THE VIEW INADEQUATELY. I TURNED AWAY FROM THE TEAM AND PRAYED FOR A MIRACLE. I GUESS IT'S ALL RELATIVE. I DISCOVERED MYSELF IN WAYS I HAD NEVER KNOWN WERE POSSIBLE—AND IT DEFINED THE REST OF THE TRIP FOR ME. THERE WOULD BE VERY FEW MOMENTS THAT TRULY MATTERED.

poles. MM was his usual livewire self. He couldn't sit still for more than a few minutes. He finally gave up and found his way to the kitchen to help make our lunch. Anamika was his ebullient self and kept the conversation lively.

As I lay there in pain, I wondered what I was truly made of. If you ask people close to me to describe my pursuit of goals, some of the common words would be 'extremely determined', 'gets to his goal always', 'leads with grit' and so on. And here I was, after half a day's trek, considering quitting. Was I actually a determined man? Was I truly strong?

My mind wandered to all the people who are true adventure-lovers. How do they do it? I had been reading the book *Into the Wild* by Jon Krakauer, which told the story of American hiker Christopher McCandless who travelled across the US and eventually hitchhiked to snow-covered Alaska where he was found dead after trying to brave the elements. I thought that most of us want to be that free spirit Christopher McCandless was in real life. But seldom does anyone truly have the courage to be that. We have a few small adventures and think we have accomplished a lot. Are we lying to ourselves? What is life? Every single person has a story, and everyone faces difficulties in life, believing theirs is the worst.

So then, what is worthwhile in life after all? I had long concluded that I could never be a McCandless. But what matters is that I do what matters to me, however small, and I was determined to continue to do so.

The painkillers finally kicked in, and because I was flat on my back on a hard surface, the muscles started to ease up. I wondered how much of this 'recovery' was because I'd decided that failure was not an option. Ultimately, like most things in life, it comes down to attitude—and this moment was no different. My attitude was positive, and I am sure that it allowed the medicines to take effect far more easily than they would have otherwise.

As the pain began to subside, I started to think more rationally. Now that I'd decided to press on, I needed to heed my doctor's advice and not carry my backpack. So I checked with our guide, and he told me that while it would cost me a little more, our Sherpa could carry the bag for the rest of the trip. What a simple solution to a problem I had magnified! Sometimes it pays to talk about a problem rather than make it a big deal in your head.

The team woke me up when the food arrived. I sat up. I certainly felt better, even if the pain had not gone completely. The conversation picked up as we ate and many topics were discussed and debated. One factor that we paid attention to was 'fatigue'. It was a word that we would get intimate with over the next twelve days, our legs already starting to feel the strain of exertion. I went into a detailed explanation of how lactic acid builds with strenuous exercise and causes muscle fatigue. While we rested, the body would process it out, and we would get back to normal. But because we were going to be exerting ourselves for two weeks straight without a break, each day a residue would remain. The body needed time to recover; if not, it would process what was possible, leaving the rest of the muscle strain to gradually accumulate. This meant that our fatigue would get progressively worse.

After an extended lunch and rest, my back felt a whole lot better. I spoke to the team about what I had just been through. While they had known about my back problems, they had not realized the intensity of it. I reassured them about it, and we decided to resume our trek. This time I was careful and handed my backpack to Ming Ma, the Sherpa who was trekking with us. It was easier without the backpack—although it hardly weighed 4 kilograms, it had caused immense harm in the morning. I remembered the words of my doctor. He had warned me that even 1 kilogram on a back with a slip disc for any period of time could be damaging. I had forgotten that in the morning's excitement. But I was determined not to do that again.

We got back on the trail. The gradient was immediately a steep ascent. I had no backpack, just my trekking poles, but a full stomach and a lack of experience in climbing steep slopes made it feel a lot worse. Looking back, of course, I think this first climb was far easier than those to come.

I guess it's all relative. You hit rock bottom, only to realize that there are many others in worse shape. Suddenly, the situation is not so bad. On the flip side, you are on top of the world and realize that many others have it even better, so you come crashing down pretty hard, pretty quick. Why do we always compare ourselves to others? Is it our social nature? Or is it that from the time you are born, you are compared to others. Even your doctor compares you to the 'standard' to determine if you are 'normal' or not.

The trek from Lukla had been downhill, as it was a trek down to the valley of the Doodh Kosi river. From there, it was all uphill. This was going to be the trend for most of our trip—a walk down to the valley, typically in the mornings, then a steep ascent on the next mountain, and a walk down to the valley again. We were following the river all the way.

The ascent took us nearly an hour and a half. We reached the top and the trail started to flatten out,

and sometime later, we reached a small town called Phakdin. Our guide Tikka had told us about this town at lunch, asking if we wanted to stay there for the night or carry on to the next town. After quite a bit of debate, we decided to pitch our tents in Phakdin for the first night.

'Phakdin'—imagine five guys in a town with a name like 'Phak Din'. Ever since Tikka had mentioned the town, Anamika had been obsessed with the name. Given its ring, everyone caught on, and this resulted in many laughs and jokes. We had so much fun with it that as a group we made our first significant decision—we were going to call ourselves the 'Phakdin Five'. True to his creative style, Anamika came up with the name, and we unanimously agreed. Many times during the day, we had cursed when the going was tough or we were in pain. Each time we wanted to curse, we decided to be 'polite' and instead of screaming 'F@#$ it!', we'd scream 'Ding it!'. So that became the natural tagline for our team—'Just ding it!'. All of a sudden we had a common identity. We were the 'Phakdin Five' who decided to 'Just ding it' with everything that life threw at us. It felt really good.

The decision to pitch our tents in Phakdin had been made after a lot of debate. I really wanted to press on so that we could make as much progress as possible. I was under the constant fear that my back would give way, and that I wouldn't be able to go on. Anamika made the clinching argument when he reminded us that we had christened ourselves the 'Phakdin Five', so we had to stay in Phakdin at least for a night. This, however, meant that the next day would be a much longer one.

Phakdin is a beautiful small town nestled in a mountain valley, on the banks of the gorgeous Doodh Kosi river. (This river originates from the glaciers of Mount Everest, and most of the trek to the Everest Base Camp is along the river.) Phakdin is nestled against the backdrop of steep mountains and cliffs and the river adds an ethereal radiance to the town.

For most of this day in April, the weather was warm and sunny, with no clouds. But with the sunset, we were going to get a rude awakening. That evening, I discovered myself in ways I had never known were possible—and it defined the rest of the trip for me.

At Phakdin, we checked into the 'Namaste' Lodge. The first thing we did was to take off our trekking shoes, put our feet up, and say 'ahhhh'. Yes, that huge sigh of relief was a simple but huge pleasure, one that we'd cherish throughout the trip. Even though I'd ensured that my shoes were comfortable and broken in prior to the trip, they got heavy after a long day's trek. So getting those 2.5 kilograms off my feet took the weight off my legs and it felt awesome.

It was about 3.30 p.m. It had been a relatively short trek for Day One, yet I felt exhausted. Since the weather was warm, I decided to take a walk to the banks of the river and enjoy an hour of peace and solitude. After a quick change into comfortable shoes, I walked to the river. The rest of the gang decided to do the same except Pappu. He felt exhausted and decided to relax in the room. This caused a little disappointment since we were planning a full segment for my video journal where we would introduce the Phakdin Five in Phakdin. We now had to do that with just the four of us.

The riverbank was a mass of rocks and boulders. My first taste of the cold was when I decided to dip my toes in the water. It was freezing—the river was melted water from the Khumbu glacier on Mount Everest. This reminded me of the spring in Chicago where the weather would be bright and sunny, creating the impression that it was a gorgeous day, but actually, the temperatures were below zero.

As I sat on the banks of the river, I felt at peace. What is it about water that makes things feel different?

What makes water give us so much peace? Is it that life originated from water? At a subliminal level, our attraction to water is very strong. The shores of a sea, the banks of a river, the winding paths around a lake all make the mind calm. When the mind is at rest, one can think clearly without any clutter.

The Doodh Kosi river flowing down the mountains was no different—serene and magnificent. It was a perfect place for me to capture some of my thoughts, with the soft rumblings of the river as it slid over the rocks melodiously lulling my mind. It made me wonder if there were any sounds in the world better than the sounds of nature. I was feeling wonderful.

The sun was fast setting, and the mercury plummeted very rapidly. In less than thirty minutes, all the warmth was gone and it was beginning to get uncomfortable. My first reaction was to get back to the room lest I expose myself too much to the cold and fall ill. The others decided to wait a little longer and have that last sip of beer since drinking alcohol the next ten days, when we would climb higher altitudes, was not recommended. Alcohol leads to dehydration, and the possibility of poor coordination makes it dangerous.

I got back to the room and rested. Later, we met in the teashop or 'restaurant'. An early dinner was on the cards, around 6.30 p.m. We didn't know it then, but this would be our schedule each day of the trip—early start, long days, exhaustion, early dinner, and sleep.

We had completed Day One successfully. All of us were in great spirits and the conversation at the dinner table was interesting. We discussed almost every topic under the sun, from the good to the bad and the ugly. As our conversation progressed, the other Phadkin Fives commented that I would not shut up. They did acknowledge, though, that they learnt a great deal over the course of the day—from facts on business to trivia on theology and other varied topics. I was that guy in the group who kept up a stream of information coming their way, whether they wanted it or not. Most of the information was not relevant, but it certainly was interesting (or at least I believed so).

In response to one of my long-winded explanations on yet another random topic, I got one of the best back-handed compliments from MM when he called me 'transformatively disruptive'. I am not sure he meant it as a compliment but I took it that way because my explanation had bordered on the ridiculous. So it definitely brought a smile to my face.

Over the years, I have realized that I cannot think in a linear manner on any topic even if I tried to. I think laterally. More often than not, I don't even stop there, but go on to question the fundamental premise of an idea each and every time. I call this tangential thinking since I am almost always on a tangent to everyone else. This fact, that I am different, is something I've had to consider throughout my life. I'm not sure if I have been this way since childhood. All I know is that in both my personal life and professional life, it has caused me a lot of angst. I have spent many a night thinking about this trait and how I can and must change it. But when I have attempted to change, I have not been able to. Over time, I had to start asking myself if I should change. Being the odd one in a crowd takes its toll on anyone and I can feel the pressure of this every day.

MM works in what the world refers to as 'analytics'. As the conversation proceeded, he asked me what I thought about the world of analytics. True to my nature, I went off on a rant about how it was simply repackaged hogwash that's been getting recycled every couple of years for the last twenty years. It was simply the basics of any business operation retold with new buzzwords to keep consultants busy and give the corporate world something to look forward to and talk about to their boards and executives. Other than MM, the rest of the team was in splits. I don't think he was amused, considering I had just trashed his profession. Later, I realized that I'd been extremely insensitive. At times, I'm far too blunt and candid, something that I need to work on.

While I spoke without thinking, MM's primary trait was over analysing every detail. He'd analyse even a simple joke for hours after it was delivered, letting the thought or conversation linger in his head for so long that we ended up naming him 'MM' or 'Mental Masturbation'.

When friends sit around a dinner table and bond well, topics of conversation could be anything, and time flies. Food tastes good and drinks feel wonderful. This was one such evening, the culmination of a good day of trekking, lots of learning, and simple food. In a moment of reflection, I thought that if we were to look back at the last few years of our lives, there would be very few moments that we'd remember and fewer moments that truly mattered. Most memorable may be moments that define our lives, mostly those we've spent with family or friends, whether happy or sad. As social animals, human beings perhaps find most happiness with people close to them. Don't get me wrong—each of us wants and needs solitude regularly, but there's no substitute for a caring family and group of friends. Yet, in the mad rat race of the world that we live in, we never find time for what truly matters.

The sun had long set by the time we headed back to our rooms, and it was then that we realized that it was bitterly cold outside. As we left the comfort of the heated main room of the teahouse for our own rooms, we shivered in the cold. I have lived in the windy cold winters of Chicago, in the frozen tundra of Minnesota, and on the icy shores of Lake Michigan so I assumed I could manage cold weather pretty well. What I had not factored in was that in each of those situations, I'd had the luxury of a heated car or home or building to run into. Here, I had nothing. This was the first time I was experiencing absolutely no heat.

What made it worse was that there was no electricity. The cold and pitch-darkness added to the freezing effect. We had three double rooms for the five of us, and I was the loner that night, with a room to myself. I felt like the cold was biting into every inch of my body, which began to ache with the cold. I was already wearing many layers of clothing, but I pulled on more thermals in the hope that it would warm me up. Nothing seemed to help, and I panicked.

What I did not realize was that it takes the time to warm up. But when one panics, patience disappears. The only silver lining was that my phone was working intermittently; so I called my wife. She had a lot of experience in mountain climbing, and she was matter-

of-fact, telling me to wait for my body heat to warm me up, it would take just a short time. That was an extremely reassuring phone call.

The natural reaction of the body to cold is to become stiff. And stiff muscles would result in back pain. Sure enough, my shoulders and back started to feel like they were splitting. It felt like the afternoon all over again. Enduring this much pain once again on the same day was eroding my mental strength. I was fighting a losing battle trying to resist the urge to quit. The silence and loneliness in the room were not helping. I tried to remind myself of the old adage that adversity builds character. In fact, I told myself that day that adversity was not building character—it was revealing it. I had to be strong. I had to lie down flat, so I pulled out the sleeping bag liner and tried to settle in. My teeth were still chattering loudly and my body was still shivering. After a lot of effort, owing to the clumsiness brought on by frozen limbs, I managed to zip myself into the liner and got the thick blanket on me. I lay there flat just praying to God to give me the strength to fight this situation now and in the future. As I lay there, I began to reconcile myself to accepting the possibility that I may not be able to continue with the trek. If the first night was this bad, I could not even begin to imagine how much worse it would get as we moved further up. My mind veered between calling myself a loser and reassuring me that quitting did not make me one.

All of a sudden, I realized that my pain was easing up, my body had stopped shivering, and I was feeling a lot better. It was definitely warm inside the liner. As my body felt more comfortable, I began to think about how easily—within a few days of knowing me, in fact—MM had described me as being transformatively disruptive. Just recently, I'd gone to see one of my mentors, and he had told me to be true to myself. That ultimately, that's what mattered, and that's what would work: 'Don't ever lose your individuality.' MM's comment had definitely opened up my insecurities, and made me question if I should change—and whether I had the courage to face the world despite being 'different'.

In the darkness, I reflected on my life. As I had moved up in the corporate hierarchy, there were times when this tangential thought process had won praise. But far more often, my thoughts had been ahead of the moment or time and were rejected, and I got tagged as 'immature' or 'childish'. So there was a constant conflict between who I am and my desire to be accepted for who I was. This resulted in a wide arc of emotions, from desperation and sadness to elation and bliss.

It had been a good day. It was a first for me in many regards—but I did not realize that it would be the first of many days of acute introspection for me. As it got warmer inside the sleeping bag, the excitement of the day and the exhaustion of the trek got the better of me and I slept.

TWELVE

DAY THREE
Setting goals

MEDICALLY, EMOTIONS ARE JUST secretions of hormones. But do we truly know what they are? In simple terms, emotions are what define life for us every day. Imagine if we had none! Most ancient books, especially the religious ones, advise detachment from all 'worldly' pleasures or emotions. How many can truly do that? Do we want to? We enjoy the highs and it's the lows that help us enjoy the highs even more. How would we know there was light, if we did not know what darkness means?

My physical and emotional weariness ensured I slept soundly. When I woke up, it was cold, but putting last night's panic behind me, I was much better prepared to face the day.

I decided to check in on the others. My first surprise was that Anamika and MM were already awake and in deep conversation in the adjacent room. Anamika had injured his ankle the previous day, and it had swollen up over the night. He was in a lot of pain and hadn't been able to sleep. I took a quick look; there wasn't any injury to the bone, so it had to be a sprain. My first reaction was to get him some painkillers to lessen the pain and then to immobilize his ankle. I was upset that he'd spent the night in pain and disappointed he hadn't told anyone—we could have dealt with this sooner, and he might have felt better by the morning. Plus, he had potentially ruined the entire day for himself by being considerate and letting all of us sleep as he suffered through the night. Either way, we had some tough decisions to make, the foremost being whether Anamika wanted to continue, given that we weren't sure how long the ankle would take to heal.

For his part, Anamika gave us a resounding 'yes' to pushing on. So we needed to decide if we should carry on at the cost of compounding the injury; whether Anamika should stay back until he was better and then catch up; or whether we should all wait for him to improve. We had a discussion with Tikka, and he gave us the option of getting a horse. Anamika could ride it that day and rest his ankle.

That Anamika was in a lot of pain was evident from his face. But his attitude was fantastic. I have written about attitude being the lynchpin of any difficult undertaking such as this journey. Injury or trouble or potential disruption did not darken his spirits and his mood remained positive. I did not realize how much I appreciated the attitude until the next morning.

We decided that Anamika would ride while the rest of us trekked up to Namche Bazaar. The facilities there were much better, and we could even get him some medical help if needed. We decided to defer the decision on whether he would continue for the rest of the trip until then.

It was a cold morning and we decided to layer up in full gear to stay warm. We were all city boys who'd only read about life in the wilderness, never experienced it. Now that we were trying to live it, overcompensation and caution became the norm.

This made me reflect on 'experience'. We grow older day by day, and, it is said, wiser. Wisdom comes naturally from the enormous amount of knowledge that we gain through everyday actions, not necessarily just by reading or studying. This knowledge becomes an experience and helps us handle life. While we never stop to think about this, we are smarter today than we were yesterday. When a situation is tough, experience helps us deal with it. But that morning, I realized how much I took life for granted and how there was a lot I have to be thankful for each day.

Breakfast was simple, but good—omelettes and toast with hot tea. I was just thankful that we didn't have to rely on cereal bars or snacks. A little later, we were all set to leave. Tikka had arranged the horse by then. We lifted Anamika onto it and he set off, saying we would meet for lunch.

Friends who had trekked to Namche Bazaar had warned me that it was among the toughest and longest climbs. Even so, I was looking forward to Day Three's trek, and so, it seemed, did the others. I felt energized after a good night's sleep, which had helped my muscles recover fully and the others, too, felt the same. We didn't realize that this feeling would rapidly disappear. But I guess it's this uncertainty of the future that makes life interesting. If given a choice, would I want to know everything about the future? Maybe some parts of it, but certainly not every detail.

We got back into our trekking shoes, picked up our trekking poles and day bags and began our trek from Phakdin. We made steady progress, and it was a quick climb up from the Phakdin valley into the rhododendron and magnolia forests. I'd hoped to catch the flowers in bloom—I'd read about their beauty while researching—but it was early in the season, and there were only a few in bloom. We managed to click a few pictures to prove it!

As we continued our climb, we were greeted again with the sun shining brightly in the sky for the second day in a row. Soon we hit the classic winter conundrum. As I began to climb, the multiple layers of clothing that I was wearing became redundant. Slowly but surely I started peeling them off. I felt brave that I was managing the cold really well. But the first hint of wind reminded me that it was freezing, and I started to worry about whether I was risking exposure and would fall ill. So the conundrum remained—stay layered and sweat it out, or worry about falling sick and not making it to the end. This played out in my mind for the rest of the morning and was more or less the same story for many days of the trip.

As we trekked up the mountains, the views astounded us with their beauty. We were walking along the Doodh Kosi, gaining altitude steadily. The valley and the sheer cliffs on either side were gorgeous—it was nature at her best and conducive to introspection.

'Doodh Kosi Nadi', as the river is called in Nepal, is one of the hundreds of rivers that originate from the Himalayan glaciers, its source is on Mount Everest. The water is pure and pristine white, just like milk, and hence the name 'doodh' or 'milk' in Nepali.

I stared at the river meandering down the mountain. Like a human being, a river is inherently beautiful, pristine and pure at birth with no malice, no good, just pure innocence.

Throughout the early stages, the flow is slow like a baby learning to stand, crawl and then run while taking in the surroundings. As it makes progress, it continues to look forward to the journey of life. Like a baby, the environment dictates the flow of the river. The path it takes is a direct result of the resistance that it gets from various external factors.

In its youth, it is vibrant, provides sustenance and life to living creatures and is an absolutely positive asset to everyone. Then there are times it becomes destructive and causes hurt and unhappiness. Like humans, a river that has a predilection for trouble or destruction has to be managed. As we manage humans through guidance and education, a 'good' river is a boon for society. In the prime of youth, it is full of momentum and skips through life. Before it realizes, the river gets 'old'. It carries with it the 'responsibilities of life' and all the 'qualities' that it has picked up. Soon enough the cycle of crawl, walk, and run reverses.

Towards the end of their lives, like the humans realize that they have to get rid of a lot of 'unwanted baggage' they have collected, the river starts to shed its weight and small deltas and islands are formed. But the innocence and purity that it started with is never regained.

In the end, whether it is a river or a human, we all merge with the sea, part of an immense bonded with all, yet pulled back or down by none.

The sound of Lifebuoy skipping over a big stone into the river recalled me from my reverie. I watched in awe as the Doodh Kosi meandered down the mountainside, gathering momentum as it neared the valley. Up there at the altitude we were at, it was in its youth, strong, vibrant, and ready to conquer the world. As it flowed down the mountains, it never seemed to worry about the boulders or obstacles it would encounter. When it did find an obstacle in the form a big rock or a fallen tree, a part of it tried to combat the obstacle, or flowed around it to continue its mission. Over time, it weathered the obstacle down and beat it. I thought that summarized the essence of our lives. There are

always troubles and obstacles. When your enemies hit you hard and stop your endeavours to 'flow', try to see if you can get around the problem. Persist, endure, and you will get what you want.

LIKE A BABY, THE ENVIRONMENT DICTATES THE FLOW OF THE RIVER. THE PATH IT TAKES IS A DIRECT RESULT OF THE RESISTANCE THAT IT GETS FROM VARIOUS EXTERNAL FACTORS.

The weather was beautiful, the mountains touched the sky, everything was lush green and dewy and the water skipped over the rocks gurgling. We were in high spirits, and so the conversation flowed easily, with jokes and banter.

We continued our trek and stopped for our first break and tea at a place called Toktok, which is approximately 9000 feet (2760 metres) above sea level. Our guide Tikka reminded us that the trek on this day was going to be a long one, so we could only afford a brief stop. The tea felt good as it went down and warmed the body. While walking, the body heat generated had warded off the cold, but now I realized how icy it truly was.

As I stepped out of the teahouse, the freezing temperatures hit me in the face. I got all my layers back on, including two pairs of gloves. I pulled out a bar of Snickers, and resumed my climb munching on it. The ascent was quite steep, and needed some effort and I could feel the strain on my calf muscles. Concentrating on the climb, we refrained from talking too much.

The sun grew brighter, and with the extra effort of the climb, I began to sweat once again. It got so warm that I started to peel off the layers and eventually got to just a half-sleeve dry-fit. I wasn't sure this was the smartest thing to do, but it was so hot that even a single piece of clothing felt too much.

My striptease provoked some good-natured humour, with MM remarking that he couldn't wait for the swimsuit round of the beauty pageant. I quickly responded that he might be better off wishing for the birthday suit one. Conversation and humour can lighten any load. Our light-hearted exchange was enough to restart the banter and our laughter made me forget the physical stress of the climb.

It is often said that one must count one's life not in the hours but in the number of times one smiles in a day. Humour is a beautiful thing that eases a lot of pain.

The mind is so amazing that it can forget almost any pain, if measures are taken to control its turbulence.

Over the next several days, we realized that MM specialized in throwaways. He'd say something so tangential that you had to really stretch your mind to connect it to the ongoing conversation. But it certainly made for entertaining conversations. The fallout was that MM became the butt of many of jokes. Something as silly as 'A Chinese, a German and an American went to a bar...' was followed by 'MM, I am sure you will analyse the joke for the next two hours'. Being a good sport, MM took most of the comments and jibes well. We'd declared him to be the official 'virgin' of the group when it came to sex or related aspects; the origins of this label came from his (feigned) ignorance of the topic of our Nasha Bar conversation in Thamel two days ago.

But as the trail got tougher, the conversation trailed off. We needed to focus on the ground, the rocks and the gaps on the trail to prevent mishaps. The ascent continued to be relentlessly steep. We were so focused on the trail that we missed the beauty surrounding us. As I trekked, I wondered if life was similar. We are all in this mad rat race and are so focused on getting to our destination or goal that we miss the big picture of life. We miss the forest for the trees many times and in the process, fail to grasp the true meaning of life.

A final strong effort got us to Monjo—a small, quaint village nestled against the mountains. We stopped at the Nirvana guesthouse where Anamika was waiting for us. He had reached the guesthouse over an hour before we did and was sketching the mountains. We were ravenous, so the food that we ordered seemed delicious. We were still at the lower altitudes, so there was apple tart on the menu for lunch! Needless to say, lunch was good, and suddenly, life felt a lot better after we ate.

As I walked out of the dining room, I glanced at the sketch Anamika was making. He'd captured the mountains and the scenery beautifully. They appeared almost real, the dark lead pencil he'd used making it look like a black-and-white photograph of the valley. It was an exhibition of really strong talent. I was in awe, and I wondered why Anamika had not pursued his creative side further. What could have pushed him away from exploring this talent and directed him to the world of finance and numbers?

How many people can truly say that they're doing what they actually want to in life? If there were no restrictions imposed on us, would we do what we do every day? The pressure to succeed in the eyes of society has driven many a talented person to pursue survival and success rather than a life with a true sense

of accomplishment. 'Doing what you like is freedom; liking what you do is happiness'. If so, very few are free; and even fewer are happy.

Although Anamika is a very successful man and has the freedom to do what the wants, he harbours regret and often wonders if he should have chosen to be an architect instead. Now that I'd seen his sketch, his thoughts made sense to me.

I inhaled the crisp air and reminded myself that every extra minute of rest meant that it would be tougher towards the end of the day. The weather was still very pleasant, and the sun shone brightly. Tikka had told us that the climb to Namche Bazaar would take approximately three hours from where we were. But so far, since we'd always taken longer than he'd anticipated, we assumed it would take us four hours, which meant that we had to start as soon as possible. But we were tired after the morning's climb and decided to rest a little more before we set off again.

The early part of the afternoon trek was along the Kosi. This time we walked along the river. Though the terrain was rocky, it was not a difficult trek as there were hardly any elevation changes. About forty-five minutes into the trek, I looked up and realized that the climb ahead was very steep. It felt as if the slope was almost perpendicular to the ground. I wondered if it was going to be this steep all the way to Namche Bazaar. My legs were protesting already.

We crossed the valley and began the climb on the other side. It was even steeper than it appeared. As I laboured hard to move my feet, I knew this was not going to be easy. For once, my friends had turned out to be right. This really was one of the toughest parts of the trek not just in terms of its physical demands but also as a test of endurance, stamina, and mental strength.

Climbing the steep incline meant that I was holding my body at an angle, with my shoulders straight and stiff. I could sense that this was a recipe for pain, but I had no other choice. In a matter of half an hour, my back started to pain and I knew progress would become slow.

The pain intensified, and I kept hoping for a flat surface and the end of the climb. Each blind turn gave me hope that the end was near but was shattered a few minutes later. It felt like the climb would go on for eternity. Each step got tougher and the pain worse. Exhaustion hit me hard and I found myself labouring to take the next step. I badly wanted to climb to the end, so I kept asking Tikka how much longer we had to go. He knew I was struggling, so he mumbled something vague instead of giving me a straight answer. I felt so exhausted that his responses did not register.

The pain grew worse with the climb, the altitude, and the fatigue. I knew I would not make it unless I made adjustments and tried different techniques. The only conversations I had, for the most part, were with myself, pushing and egging myself on. One of the techniques that I adopted was the 'math of counting'. This simple technique involved setting a target for the number of steps I would take between breaks. This proved quite effective and proved handy over the next several days.

Many of us have personalities that are goal-oriented. Modern society calls that a 'Type-A' personality. If I stick to that definition, I believe I will fall within the framework of the Type-A construct. When I have a goal that I am committed to and am passionate about achieving, I am so driven that I come across as obsessed. Each person is motivated in their own way. What drives motivation? Ultimately, it comes down your priorities and whatever gives you happiness, and satisfaction. Human beings are inherently selfish. While the word 'selfish' has an automatic negative connotation, if you were to take the word in its pure form, you will realize that human beings are selfish but not necessarily in a negative way. For example, we donate money to a charity because of the goodness of our hearts or we feel it's the right thing to do. But in that process, what we actually are doing is catering to one of our priorities and through that we gain happiness and satisfaction. The act of performing the 'good deed' gives us satisfaction—isn't that the literal definition of the word 'selfish'?

Goals are important for any person, the natural expression of aspiration. Then there are others that believe they don't need goals but still set them subconsciously. After all, a goal is an aim. Without it, life tends to lose meaning. But the degree to which each person focuses on their goals drives their personality significantly.

I felt I was about to collapse. The pain was shooting down my shoulder and radiating to my spine. I could not move. As I sat down on a rock, the fear of failure once again reared its ugly head. Tikka came over and told me that there was a comfortable resting place a few minutes ahead. As I sat on the rock and the pain started to reduce a bit, I decided that I would attempt to get to the area that Tikka had indicated. The slope of the mountain looked intimidating, but I had no choice but to try. It was a quick climb, and we reached Jorsale (Thimbug), at an altitude of 9,000 feet (2,740 metres).

This was the official entrance to the Sagarmatha National Park. Sagarmatha is the local name for Mount Everest. It means 'mother of all mountains'. The big sign at the entrance got us excited. For a moment I forgot I was in pain. The visitor's centre there had only one room, and looked shabby. Evidence of its past splendour could be seen in the pictures, lists of facts, props—but time and lack of maintenance had worn down many of the exhibits. It was a small room and several people crowded it. When I saw there was no place for me to lie down, I went outside, found a rock to sit on and leaned my back against another. The pain and the fatigue made me close my eyes. As we still had a long trek ahead to get to Namche Bazaar, Tikka soon came around to push us to move. I refused to move; I just couldn't.

I was acutely aware that we had to cover a long distance that day. But resting my back against the rocks was helping, and the pain was losing its biting edge. I'm not sure how long I had my eyes closed, but as the pain got better, I told the team we should resume our climb. From their reaction, I realized they were genuinely concerned. I produced a white lie to reassure them, but I wasn't very convincing. Without a word, we started back.

My legs started protesting as we continued the climb and my back was getting stiffer. But I wasn't sure if it was the climb that was doing this or if fear and tension were the culprits. 'A cat that falls into hot water is scared of cold water' goes the old adage. The pain over the last couple of years and the episode at the visitor's centre made me shudder at the thought of a full-blown pain attack. I had to hold myself together and make it through the day. The angle of ascent was very sharp and each minute seemed really long. As the pain increased, I became even more adamant that I would not let it stop me. I continued to push through.

After another hour, we reached a point past the Larja Bridge where one can see Mount Everest for the first time. Unfortunately, it was hidden behind clouds, and we were denied that first sight. Over the course of the next ten days, I realized that mornings are always better for views; it gets cloudy in the afternoons, making it difficult to take pictures. But the time we spent trying to discern the outline of the Everest within the clouds gave my legs a much-needed rest, and my back started to relax as well.

The afternoon trek had been so intense that each of us had adjusted ourselves into patterns that felt personally comfortable. Each of us had set an individual pace and method to accomplish the steep climb. In life this seems true as well. When the odds are stacked against us, we generally tend to adopt methods and practices that we are comfortable with.

Lifebuoy and I had been trekking ahead, while MM and Pappu were taking it slow. I didn't realize that I was keeping a relatively faster pace. I assume I was doing that subconsciously to get through the journey as fast as possible. As much as I thought I was shielding my pain from the team, they knew what my true condition was. So Lifebuoy decided to stay close to me. Over the course of the trip, I realized that he was a big man with an even bigger heart. He was concerned about me and was determined to 'assist' me whenever needed.

Lifebuoy had been close to his father ('Baba'), but had lost him just a few months earlier. Thoughts of him had been weighing on him as we climbed up. As the difficulty of the trek increased, he was regretting not having spent enough time with his father during his final years. This trek was his way of overcoming his grief and regret—in many ways, he wanted to succeed for his father.

We continued to stop frequently. As we looked back down the mountain, I saw Pappu was struggling a lot. Considering he was the most disciplined when it came to daily exercise, I wondered why he was so obviously labouring through every step. It was past afternoon; the shadows were getting longer, and sunset was near. It was going to be a race against time for me while managing the pain.

Tikka was trying to get our spirits up. He kept saying, 'Namche is just around the corner. We are almost there.' Amidst the mist of pain, his words sounded hollow to me. Our excitement levels were down and we could not even envisage our destination. There were no villages between us and Namche, so we had no choice but to push along. I was also worried about Pappu, who looked as if he would collapse any minute. By now, I'd lost all hope that the climb would end anytime soon, and so I kept counting to distract myself. We kept plodding on slowly for another thirty minutes, stopping to rest for longer and longer periods. Then, all of a sudden, we saw a sign around a corner that said 'Namche Bazaar Checkpost'. It was definitely the best gift for our fatigued legs and physically drained bodies. I had believed that having the stamina to walk 15–20 kilometres on roads would be enough for us to trek without much trouble, but that was definitely not so. The trek had been amazingly tough so far, but the trekking poles had been a huge help, and as I mentioned earlier, setting goals helped a lot. We wanted to get to Namche Bazaar, a sub-goal on our quest to get to the EBC. I was surprised that I was handling the consistent pain well. I took solace in the fact that the pain was steady, not increasing.

After a brief stop at the signage, we started off again. The incline had flattened out and we managed to make a more rapid progress. About twenty minutes later, we got our first sight of the 'bowl' of Namche Bazaar. Located at an altitude of 10,000 feet (3,200 metres), Namche Bazaar serves as the headquarters for the Sagarmatha National Park. It the largest village in the park, and is the village of the Sherpas. Nestled in a valley and shaped like a bowl, about three-quarters of a circle, it is sharply terraced, creating the impression of a massive stadium.

Based on counsel from my friends, we had asked Tikka to get us 'upgraded' rooms—hot showers and electrically heated blankets—for a few bucks more, and couldn't wait to get there. We stepped into our rooms completely exhausted. As I lay back flat on the bed to ease my pain, I couldn't help smiling. I felt as if I had accomplished something. Though I was grateful for it, I wondered what had pushed me to fight the pain, whether it was a desire to succeed or the fear of failure.

Tikka had told us that this was the last time on the trek that we could expect hot showers—or any water to bathe at all, for that matter. So a long, hot shower to relax the muscles was in order. But not before the pain eased up.

We all took long hot showers. As I stood under the warm water, I could feel some of the fatigue going away along with the dirt and grime. The shower was refreshing and my muscles started to relax even more.

Dinner in the mountains is always early. I'm not sure if it's because there's not much to do or if fatigue and exhaustion mean an early bedtime and hence an early dinner. Whatever it was, we had dinner each day around 6.30 p.m. I was not feeling hungry perhaps because of exhaustion and also feeling bloated and constipated. I was sure it was my 'famous' stomach reacting to largish meals the last couple of days.

Was I too tired to eat? Or was it simply empathy for MM's three-day-long constipation spell or Anamika's diarrhoea? Brushing aside these thoughts, I got back to my philosophy about food. It was based on an experience I had with my daughter when she was an infant. In one of the early trips to the paediatrician with her, like any parent, I complained that she was not eating enough and that I was really worried. The doctor responded, 'She is a human baby. If she wants food, she will ask or cry. Don't feed her by the clock or overfeed her. She knows when to ask'. It was profound advice that I implemented not only for her but for myself as well. I reminded myself that if my body did not want food, why force it? So a cup of steaming noodle soup was all I had for dinner that night. If I felt really hungry at night, I knew I had ample snacks to tide me over until the morning.

The weather outside had turned rough and heavy; snow had been predicted. With the snowfall, visibility was quickly reduced to a few feet. Very soon, it was a winter wonderland outside the windows and a pleasure to stay indoors. I was glad the snowfall started late in the evening once we were within the safe confines of the lodge. I could not help but wonder how I would have managed the climb in pain through snow.

I have always loved the snow. In Chicago, it snows for at least five months of the year. But winter can be lonely and depressing, because you don't see many people outside and neither can you go out. The only way to get through winter is to maintain a positive attitude. You can either choose to feel depressed for five months, or you can embrace the winter and enjoy it.

Fresh snow is like water brushing the soft sands of a beach—serene, beautiful, and refreshing. Typically, it's the days after a snowfall that can be annoying and uncomfortable. When it snows, the temperatures are always pleasant (between 0–2 degrees Centigrade), as the atmosphere gets heated mostly from terrestrial radiation. But when there is snow and ice on the ground, it gets really cold. The days following a heavy snowfall get bitterly cold. So I was wondering if our trek the next day would get cold and treacherous.

From the valley of Namche Bazaar, the mountains towered around us in all their magnificence, with glistening glaciers flowing down the slopes. While nothing was visible through the snowfall, we spoke about the beautiful view we'd had of the glaciers on our way to Namche Bazaar. We also got a full update from Anamika regarding his adventures on horseback. He'd had a pleasant trip, and was full of energy. His sprain seemed to be doing much better, which gave all of us hope that he could trek with us the next day.

Around 9.30 p.m., I retired to my room and lay on the cold bed, reflecting on the climb. We had crossed the first mark of 10,000 feet (3,200 metres) on our trip. That was exciting for sure. It had been a really tough day, and one of the most difficult we would have on the trip. How I had managed to make it,

I am not sure. But I knew that having the goal clearly carved in my mind helped.

Tomorrow was a day of acclimatization and hence we could afford to sleep in a little. The temperatures were colder than the previous night, but the $25 upgrades to heated blankets were definitely worth it. With just a couple of layers of clothing, I got under the comforter, lay down, and slept deeply.

THIRTEEN

DAY FOUR
Walking up a down escalator

DAY FOUR BEGAN as yet another beautiful day, bright and sunny. The snowfall had stopped. Namche Bazaar and the surrounding mountains were covered in snow. It was surreal: the awe-inspiring sight of the snow-capped mountains made me pause to soak in the tranquillity around. For a brief moment, I was transported to a different, magical world. Was it for moments like this that we had climbed all the way? I wondered, thinking that the day that began so positively had to be fantastic. It was a day of acclimatization. Altitude sickness, also known as Acute Mountain Sickness (AMS) or hypobaropathy, medically refers to the effect that high altitude has on the human body, caused by low oxygen levels. The symptoms are typically no different than a regular migraine or flu: headaches, partial loss of eyesight, dizziness, shortness of breath, among others. Normally the effects are pronounced at altitudes over 8,000 feet (2,400 metres), but it varies based on each person's constitution. AMS is not something that mountaineers or mountain trekkers can afford to ignore. It can cause pulmonary oedema or cerebral oedema in a short time frame and can be fatal. Most fatalities caused by AMS are when the patient ignores the symptoms. Keeping hydrated is helpful. The best remedy is to stop immediately when the symptoms appear, or even taking the precaution of going down to a lower altitude, adjusting, and then starting to climb back up. Acclimatization is strongly recommended at least after every 3,200 feet (1,000 metres) ascent.

IN MY EVERYDAY LIFE, IMMERSED AS I AM IN THE CORPORATE LIFE, AM I MISSING THE ROSES FOR THE THORNS? NOTHING CAN DESTROY IRON BUT ITS OWN RUST.

A day of acclimatization meant that we would trek for a few hours to a location at a slightly higher altitude and come back to the starting point in the afternoon. This meant that the trek would be less tedious and shorter. However, we took it really easy, and didn't get started till after 8 a.m. We modified our original plan to first visit the Hotel Everest View, the famous luxury hotel from where you can see the Everest, and the village of Khumjung near Mount Khumbila in the Khumbu region of Solukhumbu district, within the Sagarmatha National Forest. Given our late start, we had to drop Khumjung from our plans.

Energized once again after a good night's sleep allowed by the heated electrical blankets, we got our gear on and started off. The pattern was no different—on Day Four, our high enthusiasm came down quite quickly when the steep ascent from the outset quickly took its toll on us. The exhaustion of the last few days was adding up. We hadn't been able to recover from the fatigue of the previous day, and hence there seemed to be a 'fatigue deficit' that kept growing, the gaps between our spurts of energy increasing with each climb.

While physical exhaustion is caused by exertion, the mind, too, has control over the body to a significant extent. Refreshed by the surrounding scenery as soon as we started off, the spectacular views could only gladden our minds. When the mind sees beauty all around, it makes you feel better. That's what explains how patients feel worse in the hospital, and much better at home, an environment that their mind perceives as beautiful and peaceful. While there are many factors that evoke happiness, the environment around a person, especially positive emotions, is definitely one of them.

The views were magnificent—nature was at her best, the snowfall adding to the splendour. My mind was at peace, all my worries pushed to the back of my mind. The one question that repeatedly hammered in my head was, 'In my everyday life, immersed as I am in the corporate life, am I missing the roses for the thorns?'

Right at that moment, I was feeling wonderful. It had been ninety-six hours since we had started the trip and every moment had been rewarding. It had revealed a lot about my constitution and character, and given me a perspective on what truly mattered to me.

Tikka had told us that this would be a 'quick' trek. Our expectations had been set accordingly, so the actual trek felt tougher, as the incline continued to be steep. My thoughts wandered to Tikka, who had spent more than three decades helping amateurs like me make it to the EBC. I wondered if I could do what he did every day of my life. Are the fourteen to fifteen hours of work that I do in my office the same? Do I have a true destination? Every time, for example, when I had a coffee and complained that the cream or sugar was not right, have I paused to think what truly matters? Many a time we destroy ourselves because of our own characters and attitude: 'Nothing can destroy iron but its own rust. Likewise, no one can destroy a person but his/her own mindset and attitude'. Many of us fail to enjoy our life to its fullest. It takes character and attitude to enjoy what we have rather than lament about what we don't. As Helen Keller remarked once, 'So much has been given to me, I have no time to ponder that which has been denied.'

We continued the climb and paused at the sight of an airport strip. Our guide informed us that this was the Syangboche Airport. It was an unpaved airstrip that was not certified for commercial traffic and was restricted to transporting goods that are used for summit climbs of the Everest, or other mountains. Apparently, the idea of a commercial airport had been dropped for 'political' reasons. Tikka said that the announcement that the airport was on the anvil was greeted with severe protests from the villagers of Lukla and Namche Bazaar who would lose their income from catering to trekkers. Most trekkers, naturally, would prefer to fly directly into Syangboche.

Such politics is seen almost everywhere in the world. There is so much diversity between the countries of the world, yet they are so similar in this regard. I wondered if 'politics' was just a natural aspect of the social nature of human beings. There are many arguments to support the construction of the airport, including increased traffic and tourism resulting from a shorter schedule to trek to the base camp. This would have meant more jobs and money. However, the opposing camp had won the argument for now. The official rationale for halting the construction of the airport was that it was at a high altitude of 12,400 feet (3,780 metres) and hence would cause altitude sickness for many as soon as they landed. While there is no scientific data to prove this, they had prevailed, and the project status stood killed for now.

Almost all major projects in the corporate world today seem to follow the same pattern. How often is a project executed purely for its merit? Often, I feel a project is undertaken because a perception was created that it is the 'right' thing and is acted upon by leaders around the world, who make people feel that the leaders' idea is actually what the people want since it was their idea in the first place! It comes down almost always to perception.

We waited for a while as a large helicopter was landing. It was spectacular to watch it come in precisely and touch down. Unloading and loading took all of ten minutes and it was in the air immediately. In spite of having travelled for almost 18 years of my life, I am still fascinated with aircrafts landing. How these huge machines land precisely always impresses me. And as a private pilot, I know intimately what skill it requires. I can sit and watch planes landing for hours at end. Imagine: a 747-400 landing is 4 metric tons touching down at around 160 knots, depending on payload and weather. 'A pretty impressive feat' doesn't even begin to describe it.

After the helicopter was loaded and had taken off, we continued our climb to the Panorama View hotel. It was a relatively easy climb and we were there soon. The hotel was aptly named, as the views were panoramic. It was indeed what the soul needed. A 360-degree look around made me realize that I was in the middle of tens of mountain ranges covered in snow. The tallest ones seemed elusive, as if they wanted to hide behind the clouds. The views were so spectacular, like paintings on canvas that God had made in his free time or even hand carved. We were standing on a raised plateau right in the middle of a circle of mountains as if were in the centre of a circle of God's magnificent creations.

After the customary photo taking, we restarted our trek. It was a short trek this time, to the Everest View Hotel and the much-needed rest. Like all the other tall mountains, Mount Everest was covered with clouds.

The Ama Dablam peak, lower than the Everest at 20,243 feet (6170 metres), was shining against the rays of sun reflecting from its flat surfaces. We had hot green tea and Snickers and felt like we were on cloud nine. Life felt wonderful indeed.

After a short break and rest, we started our trek down back to Namche Bazaar. The descent was definitely easier, but because Tikka wanted us to do an extra hour or two of trekking to get us fully acclimatized, we changed the route a bit. Halfway to our hotel, it began to snow heavily. What struck me was that the snowfall and lack of sunshine made the trek seem a lot harder and longer. Of course, our wet clothes added to our discomfort.

Once we reached Syangboche, we decided to take a break. It was still snowing, and we were drenched. But we had energy and hence good spirits. This made for some interesting photos in the snow. High spirits meant lively conversation, and after the stress of the day before, the route today gave us some relaxation.

The continuing snowfall and our wet layers of clothes gave us an added impetus to move faster—the wetness started to seep in, which made us feel really cold. We made our way down quickly and soon were back in the teahouse. Fresh clothes and the warm teahouse made us feel a lot better.

As we sat around the table and ordered our food, I realized I was ravenous. Lunch arrived quickly and tasted wonderful. I am sure the fact that I was famished made the dal-rice and chapattis taste like the best I have ever had. Silence descended on the table as everyone ate heartily.

It was still quite early in the afternoon, and we had a lot of time on our hands. Pappu, who was feeling a bit poorly, had gone to rest. But because Tikka had asked us not to sleep—I am not sure why—we were all trying to stay awake. It was a tall order, considering we were tired and had just had a heavy meal. We were sure we would sleep if we went back to our rooms, so we stayed together in the common room, chatting easily.

The genesis of the macho man of the team being nicknamed 'Lifebuoy' happened that afternoon. He was the only one who braved a shower in the cold freezing water at Syangboche. He realized that he had forgotten his favourite bar of soap— a red Lifebuoy—and had asked Tikka to buy one. As we were lounging about in the teahouse, Tikka rushed in, wreathed in smiles and excitement. He had found a bar of Lifebuoy soap in the sparsely stocked local shops after multiple searches. Our macho man finally broke into a smile and took the package from Tikka. He opened it and looked inside. The smile turned into a frown, and he actually rejected the soap, saying he wanted a red one. Oh my God, we were in splits! It was tough to believe that he was still after a red Lifebuoy when a simple hot shower was a luxury. In our hilarity, we decided to name him 'Lifebuoy', also because it beautifully tied in with his personality— macho, and fully reliable.

Speaking of nicknames, Pappu had received his name because he was friendly, neighbourly, and adorable—a cuddly 'Pappu' in all ways. 'Pappu' is a name often used in north India to denote endearment and one look at him indicated he deserved it. The moment MM came up with it, we were all in absolute agreement. It sounded just right.

The team had a tough time coming up with a name for 'Anamika'. Is that because he was just a nice person or was it because he did not have any distinct or unique quality? He was our official digital single-lens reflex (DSLR) photographer and a good illustrator. So after a long debate, grudgingly, we settled on 'Artiiiist' with a decision to come up with something better over the next few days.

We had time on our hands, with no concerns weighing us down, so we had a lot of fun. I was given another nickname: 'Gyani Baba'. 'Gyani' in Hindi means 'learned'. Apparently, I lectured on any topic under the sun. Come to think about it, it was true. So while the team was generous and called me learned, a more apt nickname might have been 'Lecture Baba' or the 'Talkative One'.

My life is one of contrasts. Many refer to me as a polarizing figure. There are friends who would gladly give up anything for me, and then there are others who would love to find me missing from the face of the earth tomorrow. This is no different to what I feel about the world myself, in the sense that I usually don't take the middle ground. I would do anything (even extreme things) for the people I love, which has often got me into trouble. Some people exploit this quality to manipulate me as well, but I still land up helping them. As soon as that happens, their true colours are revealed, and I get hurt. There is calmness for a while and then the cycle repeats itself. I never seem to learn or want to learn. I wondered why that is so and is it even possible to change my character? Yet, overall, I am happy with myself.

As the afternoon progressed, the urge to sleep grew. We had to keep ourselves completely engaged to fight it off, so we got out our playing cards. The afternoon passed pleasantly and before we knew it, the afternoon had smoothly become evening and the sun had set. We had accomplished our goal—it was 6.30 p.m., and we ordered dinner. Our energy was spent, so we ate dinner in a comfortable silence. The rest had erased some of the fatigue deficit, and I expected a good night's sleep to help even further. I was happy that the team was holding up well.

I guess I spoke too soon. Pappu, who had trained the most for this trip, had been complaining for two days of pain and exhaustion. At dinner, he started complaining of fever and a sore throat, which made him feel so unwell that he wanted to quit. We had just gotten over from Anamika's sprained ankle and were looking forward to the next stage of our trek. This was a step in the wrong direction and somewhat upsetting.

I recalled that at one point, Pappu had given up halfway through the climb to Namche Bazaar. After a long pep talk, he had managed to pull through. This morning, I thought he was better. But it had been a tough climb for him to the Everest View hotel and back. While resting at the hotel, he'd told me that he wanted to quit. I really did not want to hear it, neither was I mentally prepared for it, and I didn't want to spoil the mood of the others either. We were all trying hard to overcome the odds and the last thing we wanted was negative thoughts.

Unfortunately, we didn't have the luxury of choice and the overall mood suddenly became sombre. This was the second difficult situation relating to health that we had encountered, but was more tricky. MM, of course, got tense, saying agitatedly, 'Call the doctor now…. call Tikka… call the insurance company.' He just could not sit down for a minute peacefully and, living up to his name 'MM' quite literally, refused to change the subject.

I had to take a step back and think. I told myself, 'We are not doctors. We are not high-altitude experts.' So in order to buy some time, I suggested that we all have dinner and defer the discussion to later. I thought this calmed matters down quite a bit. We ate dinner in silence. I did not realize until sometime later that MM was still tense and began talking nervously again. The others were worried but did not express their doubts too loudly. I then forced a collective conclusion that Pappu would have some medications and sleep. We would let the night pass and take a call the next morning. I was hoping that a good night's rest would do the trick.

It had been a day of downs. We hadn't fully recovered from the Namche climb, and the worry about Pappu and the possibility of him quitting was emotionally draining. It was difficult on each of us physically and mentally, almost as if we were walking up a down escalator.

FOURTEEN

DAY FIVE
All talk

DAY FIVE STARTED BRIGHT and early. For some reason, in spite of the warm blanket, my sleep was disturbed and interrupted. I woke up very early to noises from the adjoining room. We had two rooms; I shared one with Anamika, while the other three used the other. I went over and found that Pappu had decided to head back. I tried to boost his spirits and get him enthused, but it was a lost cause. Anamika was annoyed at his attitude, but Pappu had made up his mind. He was done, and there seemed to be no way to convince him. It felt like he had a slight fever, but I couldn't confirm it without a thermometer. I got the feeling that with Pappu, the exhaustion was mental.

This morning, I saw Pappu as someone who was definitely looking at the glass half-empty. I had known

him for a couple of years prior to the trip and he'd never come across as someone who quit. I wondered what was truly going on. All of us were physically exhausted. It had been tough so far, and we expected it to be so in the days ahead too. We could only help, encourage, and push him. The final decision was left to Pappu and we had to accept the decision. However, this put us in a bind again. We had to decide if we wanted to continue or not.

After some discussions and consultations with Tikka, we decided that the four of us would go ahead with the trek. Tikka would arrange for a Sherpa to take Pappu back to Lukla and get him on a flight back home. Ming Ma, the Sherpa who had been with us so far, would guide us in the morning while Tikka stayed back to make arrangements for Pappu. Tikka would then join us later in the day.

We spent some time to regroup and discuss. We had to get our heads adjusted to the fact that it was going to be only the four of us. We reassured ourselves that we were fine as a group of four, that we would be strong and continue to push forward. Then we got back to getting prepared for the day. We once again packed our stuff in the large duffel bag for the porters, loading the essentials into the day bags for us to carry.

We got together for our last meal together as a team of five in the common room. Because we had lost time in the discussions and decisions in the morning, we had to make it a quick breakfast. We said our goodbyes to Pappu, got our gear on, and in a sombre mood, set off from Namche Bazaar. We had taken the same route on our acclimatization climb the day before, so the route was familiar, helping us tremendously. The steep climb did not feel as difficult as it did yesterday. I wondered if familiarity always made things easier—or were we mentally overcompensating for the loss of a team member?

Just after we ascended, there was a sharp climb down to the banks of the Doodh Kosi river. I grew apprehensive immediately. Not because I did not enjoy going downhill, but a descent meant we would have to climb all the way back up at some point. Tikka had informed us that the morning trek would stretch to about three hours, all downhill. A quick look at the map indicated that we were heading down almost 1,300 feet (400 metres). The combination of exhaustion and losing a team member was weighing on us and for that moment I was myself seeing the glass half-empty. All I could visualize with dread was another long afternoon of climbing up.

We continued to make steady progress. As we turned a corner, the views changed dramatically. They became majestic instantaneously. The skyline was made up of Mount Everest, Mounts Ama Dablam, Tebuche, and

COULD LIFE GET ANY BETTER? COULD I JUST FREEZE THIS MOMENT AND STAY IN IT FOREVER? TIME AND PATIENCE ARE THE ONLY TRUE HEALERS. WE HAD TO GET OUR HEADS ADJUSTED TO THE FACT THAT IT WAS GOING TO BE ONLY THE FOUR OF US

Luptse. It was a thrilling moment—our first view of Mount Everest in all its glory. It was breathtaking! Again, words fail me.

The pristine beauty of the mountains lifted our spirits. I reminded myself that this was the reason we had come all the way to trek, and began to feel wonderful. We were having another great day with the sun shining brightly. For a moment I wondered, 'Could life get any better? Could I just freeze this moment and stay in it forever?' This oscillation between feeling low and elation was a constant seesaw throughout the trip as we faced difficulties on one side, but experienced the beauty and a sense of accomplishment on the other.

In spite of it being almost entirely downhill, the morning trek took us about half an hour longer than Tikka had expected. Climbing downhill was not easy, and we had to be extremely cautious. The stress on the knees not only made it painful but was also slowing us down. But the good part was the fact that we had energy and were not out of breath. That translated into great conversations.

As we talked, it reconfirmed for me that everyone has their own cross to bear. Each person has individual issues and problems that feel bigger than anyone else's, but learns to handle them through experience. Time and patience are the only true healers.

The last part of the morning trek was a steep climb down back towards the river, with sharp U-turns downhill. Many times I purposely went off the trail. It was risky, but gave me a silly high, even though Anamika was livid. I wondered if life is about the caution we show or the regrets we have about the chances we never take. Small things give us pleasure, so why deny myself those chances?

We stopped for lunch at the bottom of the hill in a small village called Phungi Thanga, which was really smaller than a hamlet. The timing was perfect for me.

It had been a long morning and my back had started to stiffen. I knew what to do and did not panic. Stiffness and the early stage of pain meant I had to rest immediately. I pulled my heavy shoes off, and this instantly gave me relief. And then I lay down flat on the bench with my eyes closed, waiting for lunch to be prepared. Resting there, I realized that the trekking poles were invaluable. I had always assumed that they were important for the support they provided on an ascent, but they were equally important for the descent, as they helped take the pressure off the knees. The other piece of equipment that had proved to be essential was the cover for the neck. The mountainside that morning did not have a lot of tree canopy for shade. While I was thankful that the sun was shining brightly, its light had been harsh and merciless, and I was glad that I had protection for my neck by the cover that hung from my hat.

The ease of the trek of the morning had spilled into lunch, and MM was extremely loquacious. He was in a fantastic mood and, for once, wrested the role of 'Lecture Baba' from me. He had an opinion on almost anything and wanted to express all of it, at once. Lifebuoy got animated as well, with Anamika pitching in with his quips. The conversation that ensued was one of the best that we had on the trip. Right out of the blue, MM started comparing the education systems in the West to those in the East. He was speaking so fast and with so much passion that I wondered that he was able to catch his breath at all.

I lay there, savouring the moment. It was great to be an outsider as the conversation went on. Since I wasn't usually a great listener, this was a wonderful experience. I abruptly sat up as I realized that it was not a moment to be missed and pulled out my video camera. This turned out to be a foolhardy move. It immediately made MM self-conscious and slowed him down. I had forgotten my back pain and wanted to rekindle our high spirits. So I jumped into the conversation and kept encouraging MM to talk. He was shy initially, but soon was back to being the 'Lecture Baba'. Lifebuoy pitched in and Anamika kept taunting him, providing immense entertainment. MM continued to voice very strong opinions on everything. He made assertions that were strong and then would not explain or defend them. This prompted Anamika to conclude that MM was just 'all talk and no cock'.

Our loud laughter was interrupted only by the arrival of lunch. And along with lunch came a pleasant surprise—our guide Tikka. He had caught up with us already. He had left Namche Bazaar about two and a half hours later than us and had taken only an hour and a half to cover the distance that took us three and a half hours. I realized that his stamina was natural because he had had been born in this terrain and did trekking for a living.

Over the last few days, I had concluded that having an excellent guide for a trek like ours made all the difference in the world. At the time Tikka was over fifty years old and had been on the mountains all his life. He started as a porter and after becoming a Sherpa (mountaineer), he had 'graduated' to being a guide. That was the hierarchy of the mountains and he had paid his dues at every step before he had become a guide. He was uneducated, but decades of doing his job meant that he knew the mountains like the back of his hand. But even more than this, what had stood out over the last several days was his attitude. He had a good heart and was willing to work hard to earn his living. Both Tikka and Ming Ma worked with passion and commitment, and that made all the difference.

I wondered if all guides and Sherpas were like them, whether this was the Nepali way of life. Could this be the influence of Buddhism, or was it just plain luck that we got such skilled guides? I concluded that it was a combination of all of these. It is their only means of livelihood and their reputation by word of mouth, their only marketing tool. So a good experience can translate into more customers, while a bad one can even ruin their business.

Lunch was sumptuous, and after a rest, we shared some oranges with a couple of locals. The eager way they accepted them made me realize the value they attributed to every small bit of food. At these altitudes, getting food all the way up was tough, and wasting food for them was a cardinal sin.

We started back on the trek, and as our legs got warmer, we picked up momentum. The altimeter indicated that we had about 2,000 feet (600 metres) to climb that afternoon. Our destination for the day was the monastery of Tengboche at 12,700 feet (3,870 metres). The steep descent in the morning meant that we were currently at around 10,600 feet (3,250 metres). Tikka had warned us that it was a tough climb, and we expected nothing less.

The lessons I had learned so far came in handy. My stride was slow and steady. From the start of the climb, I adopted the 100-step rule quite extensively. That is, I took a short break of thirty seconds for every 100 steps I took. This wasn't a rigidly fixed number, of course, and varied depending on the incline. But the average was around 100. When the incline was steep,

I took a break every sixty steps, and when the going was smooth, I could go a lot farther before taking a break. The idea was to be disciplined enough to carry on forward, but I believe this technique will work for most people as it establishes goals and gives satisfaction each time it's achieved. The key was to find something that could keep the spirits up and keep one moving forward.

The trek that afternoon took us about two and a half hours. We could see a steep incline ahead of us and the outline of a building. When Tikka informed us that it was the monastery of Tengbouche, it gave us some renewed energy. We spotted a mountaintop that had been sheared by the winds, and now resembled the sculptures of the sleeping lions near ancient Egyptian monuments. A pause for a couple of pictures and a final strong push later, we reached the arched entrance to the monastery of Tengbouche. Our teahouse was right across the monastery. We decided to go to our rooms, drop off our gear and shoes, and then visit the monastery.

The monastery at Tengbouche is beautiful, but relatively small. Some monks were chanting, so I sat down to listen. I could not understand the language, but it did not matter—it calmed my mind. I am a firm believer in God and the power of prayers. Over the years, I have come to believe that there is a power well beyond our understanding and even beyond the breadth of human imagination. The human mind is not evolved enough to even consider a true dimensionless world. For me, this translates to needing a form that I can visualize so that I can concentrate. While I give God a form based on the religious beliefs that I grew up with, this does not mean that other forms are not relevant or do not exist. Equally important, having a designated place of worship gives me solace, and going there regularly adds discipline to my life. As a believer, prayers provide me the channel for communication with God. As a man of science, it helps put my mind at ease.

The Tengbouche monastery was quiet, peaceful, and serene. It was cold, and as I sat down quietly in the main prayer hall listening to the rhythmic chanting of the prayers, I forgot myself for a while. There was no place for my troubles, exhaustion, or fatigue. It was a wonderful feeling. Almost all the holy books of all religions across the world agree on one thing: the mind is never still and is one of the toughest things in the world to control. Great things are achieved only when one concentrates and can control one's mind through focused concentration, meditation, and total dispassion.

As my mind relaxed, I felt the power within the monastery. It was the power to provide peace even to the most disturbed. The serene and beautiful face of the large idol of Buddha in almost any monastery I have visited around the world never fails to bring me tranquility.

After listening to the chanting, we went back to our teahouse for dinner. We had been on dal-rice for many days, so a vegetarian/cheese pizza on the menu caught our attention. Imagine a yak-cheese pizza at 13,000 feet (4000 metres)! We decided to take the chance and order it. The food tasted surprisingly good. The heater had been turned on and the room was getting warmer. Our dinner entertainment was the sight of the glorious golden sunset among the mountains. We stared on silently in awe and ate our dinner in peace.

As a rule, the average temperatures dropped as we gained altitude, and it would get really cold soon after sunset. The teahouses had wood-burning heaters; the wood for these had to be brought up from lower altitudes and was expensive to boot. So it was not commercially viable for the teahouses to keep wood burning throughout the day. Most of them burned firewood once in the evening immediately after sunset. This heated the room for several hours, and the embers remained for some part of the night as well. As it was intensely cold, we were all in multiple layers of clothing always.

Our rooms were frozen when we went to bed at night from the warmth of the common room. The walls were made of thin plywood that managed to keep the wind out, but not the iciness. It was bitterly cold throughout with no respite, so we began to call our rooms 'iceboxes'.

The weather had been pleasant during the days when the sun was shining brightly. Though the scheduled timings for the sunset was around 5.30 p.m., the waning rays of the sun made it cold by 3.30 p.m., and the wind chills were becoming progressively tougher to handle. It was so cold that even the mobile phones or any battery-operated device lost charge easily. My mobile phone could go from a full charge to empty in a matter of minutes or not have power at all. So I learned to keep the phone in the inner pocket of the innermost layer of clothing so that my body heat kept it warm. While the phone did not catch any network, it was useful as a camera.

At the end of a long day of trekking, when we were ready to pull out fresh clothes to wear, we would feel that everything was frozen. It felt like wearing clothes made of ice until the body heat began to thaw them and ultimately warm it up. Because showers were not available, we began to use body wipes. And because they were wet and cold, we needed to 'bathe' quickly.

Further, the naked body could not be exposed for more than a few minutes to the 'icebox'.

To fight the cold, it is seldom the thickness of the jacket that matters—it's the layers you wear. 'Layering' is critical in extreme cold weather. Almost always, I wore a regular T-shirt, a half-sleeve dry-fit, thermal innerwear, a flannel, two pairs of smartwool socks and two pairs of gloves, one with an inner lining and external gloves. I also had a solid head cover that covered the ears, and I had a balaclava for when it was windy. The only time any of these items came off was when I was wiping myself or changing clothes.

The bed felt the same as the clothes—completely wet. As I prepared for the night, I got into a consistent pattern fairly quickly. The first step was to get out of the clothes that I was wearing, clean myself with the wipes and put on fresh night clothes. The multiple layers of socks remained and so did the head cover. The next step was to fit into the tight sleeping-bag liner and zip myself up. Naturally, this resulted in a loss of dexterity. The sleeping-bag liner was like a large sock that fit against my body.

Once I settled into the 'sock', the next step was to get into the sleeping bag that I had laid out open on the bed. Both the liner and the bag were designed to deal with temperatures of 20 degrees below zero. With the loss of dexterity and the cold numbing my fingers, it often turned out to be extremely difficult to get into the sleeping bag and created some hilarious moments, the multiple layers of thick gloves adding to the fun. The decrease of oxygen in the air because of the altitude caused fatigue quite easily and stretched out the process—I needed longer breaks between my attempts to warm up. Each action took a lot more energy than normal.

After multiple attempts, I finally managed to pull the zippers of the sleeping bag or the 'mummy bag' (as we termed it as it was shaped like an Egyptian mummy), against the contours of my body. Narrow at the bottom and wider at the top, it fit snugly so conserved body heat. Movement inside the sleeping bag was not easy. Once I got into the sleeping bag, I'd put a thick blanket over myself as an extra layer of protection. It was an arduous process that took about twenty minutes each night. The combination of exhausted body, frozen limbs, and lack of oxygen made it seem even longer. I am sure once I was settled in, I resembled an ancient Egyptian mummy in a casket.

Once all this was done, I'd wait for my body heat to slowly start warming up my clothing and the sleeping bag. This took about fifteen minutes while I shivered to the bone. Eventually, it would become bearable, even pleasant, and the exhaustion of the day would lull me to sleep.

The liner and the sleeping bag ensured that the body heat did not escape. This meant that in another fifteen minutes, it would get warmer and I'd start feeling uncomfortable. So I'd begin peeling some of the layers off. Because I wore my gloves to bed, this was a bit difficult, as there was barely room to move. But pulling off my socks was a whole different ball game, requiring another five to ten minutes of sheer ingenuity to achieve. Coming out of the liner was not an option since this would mean a restart of the whole tedious process. After all this activity, I would settle down. It was critical that no part of the body was exposed either to the air or to the bed, as that part started to freeze. It was a comical situation trying to manage the exposure and exhaustion, and trying to sleep. We soon started referring to this as the process of 'mummification'. Each time I thought of it, I smiled.

FIFTEEN

DAY SIX
Young and dumb

THE NIGHT WAS NOT THE smoothest for me. As I fell asleep and descended into a world of dreams, I heard a steam engine starting to leave a station. The noise of the train got louder but it got stuck at the station. I woke up. In my half-awake state, I did not hear anything further. Realizing it was just a dream, I went back to sleep. Once again the steam engine started to roll—and even louder this time. I wondered what it meant.

The steam engine started up once again. Except, this time the noise was so loud that it felt like two engines combined. It was about 2.30 a.m. and I needed to rest so I could continue the trek the next day. I was upset that the dream was messing up my sleep. Then it hit me—I wasn't dreaming at all. It was the lady in the adjacent room snoring. She was really loud, and considering the walls between the rooms were thin plywood, it was as if my head was right next to hers. I did not have a choice: I knocked on the wall loudly. After a few knocks, the steam engine 'stopped at the station' and quieted down. I closed my eyes and tried to get back to sleep. As I slowly drifted back, the engine started rolling and gaining momentum as it left the station. I banged the wall again, and in the process, woke Anamika up. He had thought I was trying to get him to stop snoring. It was indeed a funny train journey. I call it 'funny', because that was the only way I could take it at that point. Being angry and continuing to swear would not have helped. I continued banging to get the train to stop and it finally did, at the cost of the lady not sleeping. I did not feel guilty and used the opportunity to get a few winks of sleep.

We had been making steady progress over the last five days so Tikka decided to tweak the plan a little. We had originally planned to get to a Sherpa village called Dingboche and rest. Tikka thought it might be a good idea trek up and see the Ama Dablam base camp and stop for the night at Pangboche. The next day we could proceed to Dingboche. This change in plan was in essence adding an additional day to our trip and more importantly more pain, imposing a greater test of physical and mental endurance. As a group, we were tired and in a lot of pain, so we decided against it. Our goal was the EBC and we did not want to add more variables. At this point, we were hoping that we had enough mental and physical reserves left to get to the EBC. So we headed straight for Dingboche.

As we struggled through the entire day, we thanked ourselves at every step for deciding not to attempt the Ama Dablam base camp. As we passed through the fork in the road towards Ama Dablam, we realized it was very steep and the decision was reinforced.

The trek in the morning was the longest we had undertaken on this trip so far. It took us a full four hours before we stopped for lunch. Needless to say, we had to stop at many places to catch our breath and rest. The trek was uphill for the most part, although many sections went downhill as well. As the fatigue deficit kept increasing, our anxiety about downhill terrain was proportionately going up. We just wanted to get to the EBC with whatever we had 'left in the tank' and any downhill trek meant we had to trek up again.

One of the lessons that had evolved out of our experience over the last six days was to take it 'one session at a time'. The climbs became tougher, the altitudes higher, the air thinner, the energy much less, the body progressively more exhausted, and the thoughts of what lay ahead became scarier. I began limiting my thoughts to what was in front of us. I did not want to think ahead. As the body pain worsened, the thought of 'what if we could not make it' crossed each of our minds many times in a day. Against these odds, determination was all we had. The dropping temperatures did not help either.

The trek was fast becoming a purely mental challenge; the mind had to control the body, which could barely handle the demands made on it. So at breakfast, I would plan and prepare for the morning trek. At lunch, I would do the same for the afternoon session. This strategy was no different to how players of a cricket team plan each session, one at a time, over the course of the five days of a test match.

The morning's trek provided plenty of opportunities for us to talk. Topics revolved around our professional experiences at work, but were limited to anecdotes rather than actual discussions about work. The last thing we wanted was to be reminded of all the work that was piling up for us when we returned. A long four hours later, we got to lunch at a quaint teahouse called Sunrise nestled in the lap of a beautiful valley. It was a single teahouse in a place called Orsho in the middle of nowhere in flat, desert-like terrain at an altitude of 13,300 feet (4,040 metres). There was no other habitation there. Perched on the edge of cliff created by a river flowing along the side, it stood amid mountains. It was a beautiful spot. The teahouse even had a sun room.

The solitary teahouse reminded me of Christmas in Chicago when winter is at its peak and temperatures are below freezing. Snow and ice keep people off the streets, the few that are out walking down State Street and enjoying the sweet smell of roasted chestnuts. Then there are the homeless, trying to stay warm in dirty woollens and sitting near underground vents. They have nowhere to go and no one to share their happiness or misery with.

About fifteen minutes prior to reaching the teahouse, I experienced a mild headache. As we settled into the sun room, my vision started to get blurred, I suddenly felt extreme exhaustion and collapsed on a bench. I immediately recognized the symptoms. They were the first signs of an impending migraine attack. I could only feel panic since most of my migraines were debilitating and usually lasted three days. I really did not want that kind of pain on top of the existing stress. The timing couldn't have been worse.

143

My vision got progressively blurry like it always did, until I could hardly see anything. I lay down and closed my eyes and began to pray for a miracle. Ten minutes or less is what it normally takes for my eyes to clear and severe migraine and nausea to set in. But it did not happen this time. I wondered what was happening, then suddenly it struck me. This wasn't a migraine. These were the classic symptoms of altitude sickness that I had read about. I remembered that altitude sickness could prove fatal if it's not addressed immediately.

I lay there, helpless. My choices were limited—I could wait it out and hope things would get better, or I could ask the entire team to walk back to a lower altitude. The natural choice was to try to give it some time and if that did not help, start walking down. With my eyes firmly shut, I lay on the bench in the sun room. I tried to deflect my attention away from the symptoms and was soon lost in thought.

As I lay there thinking about diseases and symptoms, I realized that against the backdrop of human evolution, medical science is still in its infancy in terms of understanding the human body. We are trying to grapple with the basics of what constitutes the human body. In this vein, I also strongly believe that most diseases can be treated better with a positive attitude.

If a person is strong-minded, it's much easier to cure a disease. Is that why placebos are so effective in modern medicine? How strong is the mind–body connection? It's always been a hotly debated topic, very tough to define and scientifically prove. Is it possible for the mind to be in full control over the body? The Bible does say: 'The spirit indeed is willing, but the flesh is weak'. Does this mean it's not possible to always control the body with the mind? Several ancient religious texts say that one can control anything in the world if one controls one's mind.

We spend billions of dollars globally in treating back pain, especially lower back pain, with massages, lumbar support, instruments, machines, and so on, but sometimes one forgets pain if the mind is distracted by, say, happy news? So does this mean the pain vanished or did the deflection of focus take away the pain and suffering? Perhaps suffering comes down to one's attitude.

The symptoms continued unabated and so did my panic. I was not sure why I was experiencing altitude sickness considering I had been on medication for it and had not missed a dose. Realizing the symptoms were not going away, I opened my eyes and informed the team of the situation. Their response was emphatic and decisive—they would do whatever was needed to make sure that I felt better. If that meant we had to trek down, that's what we were going to do. I told them that I was going to lie down and wait it out for another half hour. Tikka also agreed that rest was the best course of action. If things did not improve, we would decide what best to do.

The team ordered lunch. I had some standard painkillers as the headache was getting worse. I was semi-conscious and was listening in part to a heated discussion about the mind–body connection. Strong arguments were being made between MM and Anamika on the control that the mind truly has over the body.

Then the headache began easing up, and by the time lunch arrived, I was starting to feel a lot better. When I told the team, the relief was palpable on their faces. We decided that we would push forward, albeit very slowly. Altitude sickness can be dangerous and even fatal, if ignored. I was acutely aware of this yet something in me defied it, feeding on the hope that the symptoms would go away soon. I wondered what would have happened had I not been on Diamox, the medication to prevent altitude sickness, and how severe the symptoms would have been then.

Lunch was the staple dal-rice, and I pecked at it. Between nausea and headache, I did not feel like eating though I was hungry. Lunch was dominated by discussions on altitude sickness. Given my situation, we took an extended lunch break so I could get a little more rest.

Since we had climbed down quite a bit in the morning, we had to regain all the elevation, and more than 1,650 feet (500 metres) on top of that. It was a steep climb. My head was still aching and I felt very exhausted. I was quick to realize that only a good lively conversation would get us through the afternoon and provide a distraction during a difficult, painful and monotonous climb. I reverted to my comfort zone of being the 'Lecture Baba'. We spent an hour talking about my experiences as a leader. I told them about one of the interesting weeks of my life as a leader. The story goes thus. As the leader of over 10,000 people at that point, I got word of terrorist threats against our firm. It was a stormy time as I was a single parent for that week, my daughter was seriously ill, and my dog had cut himself and was bleeding for a long while. The US and Indian security agencies descended on my firm and demanded my undivided attention. There was widespread panic amongst our employees as the press leaked the news in the morning papers. I was also informed that I was on the 'hit list'. But I could not show any sign of panic or weakness, lest I create more hysteria among my employees. So I experienced

fear both for myself and for the safety of the people I was responsible for.

Meeting after meeting and decision after decision followed. I had to go with my gut instinct as information was scarce. I had to rally the team and keep their morale up and fear down. As I look back at it now, I believe I did well. We worked through the week and beyond to ensure that every single person was safe. And I did not neglect my daughter and her illness either. The dog did just fine as well.

Stories and anecdotes continued and pretty soon it was about operational issues that Lifebuoy and I faced every week at work. There are days I think I could write a whole different book on those and appropriately title it 'Stupidities that people do'. That got us through two hours without anyone realizing the passage of time or the steepness of the climb. I had achieved what I set out to do—to engage the group—with ample help from Lifebuoy.

AGAINST THESE ODDS, DETERMINATION WAS ALL WE HAD. I STRONGLY BELIEVE THAT MOST DISEASES CAN BE TREATED BETTER WITH A POSITIVE ATTITUDE. CONTROLLING THE MIND IS TOUGH BUT IT CAN BE THE ANSWER TO ALMOST EVERY PROBLEM.

I wondered why we don't realize the passage of time when our mind is occupied. The mind is so powerful, but human beings do not really understand it. Almost any pain or any emotion can be overcome if you focus your mind on something else. Controlling the mind is tough but it can be the answer to almost every problem.

As we took a brief rest, we looked at each other and realized we were in good spirits, so we decided to continue. My headache had almost disappeared and I was thankful for that. All of a sudden, MM suggested that each of us should reveal the most stupid thing that we had done in our lives. This turned out to be a great idea and got us laughing uproariously. MM himself started the conversation off with his messed up attempt at 'confessing love' in high school. The next anecdote was about Lifebuoy bashing the teeth out of a hotel guest in his previous job. Many stories were shared, but Anamika was quiet for a while. Then he told us about his college life, how he had been the 'bad ass' and had lived it up, defying the rules and even the law, until finally, he got arrested, but then conveniently used his 'diplomatic immunity' card as the son of a diplomat and walked out. His confession was the best thirty minutes of all and he concluded by summing up his youthful years up from the famous Hollywood line, 'Young, dumb, and full of cum'.

It was a fun afternoon that made for some wonderful moments that will remain with us forever. The trek that afternoon was nearing completion. A final push got us to our destination for the day, Dingbouche at an altitude of about 14,500 feet (4,440 metres). The sun had set and the temperatures had plummeted. We checked into the Snow Lion lodge. The room, as always, was an icebox.

As we walked to our rooms to settle down, we hit one of the grosser moments of the trip. The closer we got to our room, the stinkier it got. The stench was so strong that I thought I would faint. We looked around and realized that it came from the trekking shoes left outside a room. The sweat had developed over several days inside multiple layers of socks and had become nasty. We had two options in front of us. Either we changed our rooms or used the powder we had, which is what we did. A lavish amount of powder thrown on the offending shoes reduced the stench to tolerable levels.

The restrooms of the lodge were outside the main building, which meant we had to walk outside in the cold and relieve ourselves with about six layers of clothing on us. The saving grace was that there was a western-style toilet, so we did not have to squat.

Tikka told us that we could get a cell phone signal if we walked for ten minutes. The afternoon attack of altitude sickness had made me nervous. If I could get a signal, I wanted to talk to my doctor back home. So Tikka, Anamika, and I stepped out into the cold. The walk turned out to be about thirty minutes and the signal was spotty. However, I did manage to talk to the doctor briefly and he reassured me that I was okay.

The temperatures had dropped quite a bit by this time and the wind was so strong that Anamika's phone stopped working. I learned the technique of blowing hot air into the base of the phone to make it work from him that day. He spent quite a bit of time heating his phone up to get it to turn on. The calls had to be brief given the phones were not holding charge for long. He let his folks know that we were safe and that we were not expecting any signal for the next three days.

The thirty-minute walk back to our lodge felt like an hour as the wind was blowing hard and right into our bodies. The exposed areas of the body became like icicles, and we hurried to get back into the comfort of the common room of the lodge.

Medications and pills had become as constant an intake as food. Sitting down at the table at the lodge, I ordered dinner. The only food that I felt was safe and good for my stomach from the limited choices was dal-rice. Dinner was early, but it was a night when we had the luxury of staying up late if we wanted to. The next day was another acclimatization exercise. Seeing that it was a day to adjust our bodies to the altitude, we were planning on starting late, around 8 a.m.

As I sat at the dinner table, I felt that, overall, it had been a rewarding day despite the setbacks. I had the determination and fortitude to fight through the altitude sickness and early symptoms of frost bite on three toes. I felt fulfilled because through each high and low in the emotional rollercoaster of the day, I felt thankful for everything I had in life. With a surge of hope that I could make it through the next three days till we reached the EBC, I retired to the icebox for the night.

SIXTEEN

DAY SEVEN
The Purple Anamika

I WAS SLEEPING VERY SOUNDLY when I was woken up by loud noises from the adjacent room. The walls were thin, and I'm a light sleeper, so whoever was trying to wake their roommate up to open the door woke me up as well. It was a really cold morning, but Anamika was sound asleep in the icebox, snoring rhythmically. The sun had risen and as I sat up and looked out the window, the view that greeted me was awe-inspiring. The mountains looked beautiful and majestic with glistening snow and ice reflecting the radiant golden rays of the sun.

I had a couple of hours before we had to get moving for the day I so decided to catch up on my journal and update the video journal. As the day started on a high, I hoped it would turn out to be a wonderful one.

The rest of the team ambled out of bed and all of us assembled in the common room of the lodge. After the standard breakfast of toast, eggs, and green tea, Tikka informed us that we were going to be trekking for only about three hours. We wondered if that meant five hours for us, or if he really meant three hours.

We decided that we would leave by 8 a.m. and come back in time for lunch. Relaxed, we took time over breakfast, discussing everything from particle physics, the string theory, and unified field theory to the fundamentals of work and life. A look at the watch indicated 9.45 a.m. and we got back to our rooms to get bundled up and started on the day's trek.

On this day too, we encountered the 'hot–cold' paradox. We had worn multiple layers of clothing and were greeted yet again with a bright sun. A few minutes into the brisk trek, the body heat generated got us sweating profusely. All those areas that were exposed to the elements were freezing while those wrapped in layers of clothes were drenched in perspiration. This put even more pressure on the body and added to the overall exhaustion and aches.

With the increased sweating, I started to take off a few layers, and like always, Murphy's law had to kick in. The winds picked up and I started to feel cold again. So I had to stop and get the layers back on. This continued to be a constant tug of war that I fought throughout the trip. There was never a solution and hence I had to put up with the inconvenience.

Every day, as I started from the lodge, I felt energized after the rest at night. It did not take long for that feeling to vanish and fatigue to set in. Small and easy activities were becoming progressively tougher. Both the reduced oxygen in the air and the fatigue deficit were adding up.

The incline smoothened out and we let out a sigh of relief. The conversation that had petered out because of the gradient now picked up. We talked about how we had a nickname for all the members of the team except one, and that we had not had an official 'naming ceremony' yet. Each of us had been named after a distinct characteristic except for our 'Artiist'. We concluded that he needs to be called 'Anamika', which loosely translates to 'the one with no name', or 'anonymous', in Hindi. This was better than 'Artiist' but did not feel right. The one thought that crossed my mind is that he had an odd fascination for the colour purple. He even had a distinct pair of purple pyjamas. So we officially christened him the 'Purple Anamika', a name that I was sure would stick to him for a while to come. For his part, he was pretty explicit about his distaste for the name, suggesting 'Nasha Boy', the 'one that causes addiction'. The more he resisted, the stronger our conviction became. We stuck to 'Purple Anamika'.

We had a good steady trek for about ninety minutes and got to the valley of Chukhung at an altitude of about 15,500 feet (4,730 metres). The valley was open, beautiful and had some of the most magnificent views of the imposing mountains—Lobuche, Cholatse, Tabuche, and Ama Dablam. Tabuche is one of the fourteen peaks in the Himalayan ranges that are over 26,000 feet (8,000 metres). Tenzing Sherpa and Edmund Hillary, the first people who climbed to the summit of Mount Everest in 1963 practised on Tabuche before attempting Mount Everest. The local Sherpas and regular mountaineers consider only the mountains that are over 26,000 feet (8,000 metres) as true mountain climbing; the rest they deem as amateur trekking. We stopped and waited to take some magnificent pictures.

I found a flat surface on a rock and sat down. The valley was empty and devoid of any life. The only sound was of the wind blowing. The silence was beautiful. I had to ask myself yet again if this was what life was all about—sitting amongst some of God's most beautiful creations in a perfectly tranquil world. There was no place for worry in my head. Could life get any lovelier?

As I looked around, it was dry and without vegetation, rather like a desert interspersed with rocks. It reminded me of the pictures of the surface of the moon. A beautiful stream was flowing past, and Tikka said it joined the Doodh Kosi at some point downstream. Beautiful rocks that had weathered millions of years of erosion stood strong. The mountains wreathed in mystical charm surrounded us. It was peaceful.

Tikka came over to offer me an orange. The orange was really cold, as if it had just been taken out of a refrigerator, and was refreshing. Tikka asked us to leave the orange peel in a heap on the ground for the yaks to eat.

We spent a few more minutes enjoying nature and then decided it was time to get back to our lodge. The trek felt easier, as it was downhill for most of the way. This time, the slight breeze that was blowing kept us at a perfect temperature, not too hot and sweaty nor cold and freezing. As if it was reflective of the weather, our spirits were high as well.

As we got closer to our lodge, we saw an American family who we had met earlier in the lodge at

Tengbouche. The parents had come along with their three kids aged eight, eleven, and fifteen. Emma was the eight-year-old daughter and the other two were sons. As we spoke to them at Tengbouche and spent some time now with them, I realized they were a family of adventurers. A couple of months back they had gone extreme skiing in Greenland. Prior to that they had gone rafting, trekking, and mountain climbing. Emma impressed me the most. She was trekking all the way to the base camp and had one of the best attitudes that I have ever seen in a person. She did not attend regular school and was being home-schooled. Her parents believed that travel and a 'real-world education' would serve her much better in life than formal education, so she accompanied them as they went around the world.

MY MEMORIES ARE ONLY OF THE WONDERFUL CAMARADERIE, MOMENTS CAPTURING LIFE IN A CAPSULE THE WORD 'TEAM' WAS BECOMING MORE IMPORTANT EVERY DAY OUR MENTAL STRENGTH WAS FADING WITH THE INTENSE PHYSICAL PAIN. THIS TRIP WAS CERTAINLY NOT FOR THE FAINT-HEARTED.

It definitely made me think about this philosophy. Is this how the world should be rather than the structured schooling children go through? Does this kind of schooling constrict the thought process? Children are born free and unencumbered, yet from the moment they are born, we force them into a structured thought process and define what is right and wrong, based on many factors including our value system and our experiences. But can a totally unstructured framework be the right answer? Aren't there fundamentals like discipline that all children must have? I concluded the best answer would perhaps be a combination of the two.

Emma knew every city, town, great mountain climbers and showed an impressive knowledge of the world. Needless to say, I was amazed that an eight-year-old knew all this and more importantly, was trekking up to the EBC. Wow!

Each one of us experienced the effects of altitude sickness at some point during the journey. Today was MM's turn. He complained of severe headache, pressure on the forehead, and loss of vision. This time we knew exactly what the symptoms meant and did not panic. Learning from the previous experiences, we gave him the right medications and ensured that

he lay down with his eyes closed. About an hour later, he felt better. While not out of the woods, he was definitely looking and feeling better. I am sure it helped that we were not climbing and were staying at the same altitude.

Lunch was the usual dal-rice. It was relaxed and I looked forward to a lazy afternoon. I knew I was not supposed to sleep but at least I could rest.

The afternoon turned out to be fun. We spent time bundled up in the lodge's common room playing card games. There were a lot of jokes, yells of 'cheating', 'fouls', and friendly arguments. It was certainly relaxing mentally. I can't remember who won, who lost; my memories are only of the wonderful camaraderie, moments capturing life in a capsule.

Despite the rest, exhaustion was becoming serious and the struggle to keep the body moving was becoming harder with each passing hour and step. At the same time, the word 'team' was becoming more important every day. Each of us were trying to ignore the aches and pains, but with little success. We were trying to stay mentally strong. And each time one of us was feeling weak mentally or physically, the rest of us would encourage him to snap out of it.

The increasing exhaustion came back as a topic of discussion many times. We remembered Pappu leaving us on Day Two over a fever. Part of me was still disappointed in him for quitting without trying to live up to what I believe was his fullest potential. In our disappointment and anger, we nicknamed this attitude 'Pappu fever', so every time we were lazy or did not have the will to keep going, any complaint of exhaustion was greeted with 'Are you having Pappu fever?'

We continued to egg each other on, positively or negatively, through assurances or back-handed compliments. We were pushing each other to have the courage and the determination to reach the base camp. Anything short of reaching the base camp was a failure in our minds. When we signed up for this trek, we knew that it was not going to be easy. Despite that, not only were we unprepared, we were struggling. The mind could only overcome matter for a limited time, and from a physical standpoint it was getting increasingly difficult. Our mental strength was fading with the intense physical pain.

I spent some time meditating to focus on myself. I had to be strong. I had to carry on with my 100-step rule; I had to focus on the now instead of borrowing trouble. I had to be patient with my body and always

keep a positive attitude. I had to do whatever it took to keep my mind away from the aches and pains. In short, I had to do whatever it took to get us there. The meditation therapy session got my energy flowing, and I felt much better.

Come to think about it, this wasn't much different from 'regular life'. Facing all challenges head-on with grit and determination is an essential requirement. It isn't about never giving up—life is not about 'Pappu fever'—it's about how to work around the obstacles or through them, if needed. It's certainly not about waiting for the storm to pass; it is about dancing in the rain.

The more I thought about it, the more I was sure that everything in life comes down to attitude. As is always said, you can choose to see the glass half-empty of half-full, the choice is entirely yours. We often hear of stories of heroism or extreme resilience and in each situation, it is attitude that has played an important role.

We carried on with our card games. MM still continued to wrestle with altitude sickness, but he was an active participant that afternoon. I think this helped him keep his mind off his altitude sickness. The lazy afternoon passed by pretty quickly, soon it was time for dinner. We kept the conversation alive till 7.30 p.m. so that we would not feel sleepy.

It had been a good day, a day to refocus my mind on success; to reflect on the realities of life and on the all-important ingredient in life—'attitude'.

As we wrapped up dinner and headed to our rooms for the night, we agreed jointly that this trip was certainly not for the faint-hearted.

SEVENTEEN

DAY EIGHT
Belief and determination

IT WAS A COLD NIGHT. The mercury dipped to about 15 degrees below zero. However, I slept peacefully in the warmth of my body heat inside the icebox. It was early when we all woke up for the day's trek. This day was expected to be a long one with a trek up to Mount Lobuche at an altitude of 16,500 feet (5,000 metres). That meant we were going to attempt a net elevation gain of about 1640 feet (500 metres). Yesterday's meditation had motivated me to begin the day full of belief. So in spite of the aches and pains, I believed I was going to make it to Lobuche.

As we stepped out of the lodge, we were greeted again with a bright shining sun. The early morning rays were kissing the beautiful snowclad peaks of Ama Dablam and Amphu Gyabjen. I felt mentally prepared for the trek. The climb would be gradual and not too steep. With the wind blowing across our faces, we traversed through the Thokla valley and Dusa village until we got to Thokla (or Dughla), which is at an elevation of around 15,200 feet (4,620 metres). We made steady progress and the trip through the valley felt like we were trekking through a barren cold desert devoid of any vegetation.

It was during our trek through the valley that we were introduced to the concept of the 'Nepali toilet'. This was the term that the locals used for answering the call of nature behind a rock. Because the toilet facilities and infrastructure are absent in the mountains, this was the only option, especially useful for Anamika as he was still suffering from diarrhoea.

As we wound our way through the valley, we came across a wonderful lady from South Africa. We had met her for the first time on Day Two and had been seeing her at different times every day after that. She was a cancer survivor and was attempting to climb the summit of Mount Everest to raise money for cancer research. She told us all about her fight against the deadly disease. She was still on treatment and winning the fight for now, though she wasn't sure if she would relapse. Meanwhile, she was determined to make every day she had in this world count.

I was impressed. What an inspiring attitude! It was indeed a noble idea. Imagine the determination, the hardships, and the endurance she must have gone through as she fought the disease. Imagine the mental grit, and most importantly, the attitude. Against this attitude, all of a sudden, all my aches, pain and complaints felt trivial. She was absolutely determined to reach the summit, but how she managed to breathe in the thin air and get enough energy to move forward, never ceases to amaze me. I can only attribute it to belief. Even a simple bout of influenza brings me down for days, and here she was taking on the toughest challenge head-on. Wow! I realized belief can indeed move mountains or at least, conquer them.

This incident took me several years down memory lane when I was on an eleven-day white water rafting trip down the Salmon river in Idaho. It was a trip that was as difficult as this trek. It was extremely dangerous with Grade 4 (rating according to the level of difficulty) rapids (even some Grade 5) and hard work every single day. There were no amenities, not even the basics. It was eleven days in harmony with nature. Of the group of twenty, one man stood out for me. One of the most enterprising people I've across, he was doing the entire trip not on a raft but in a tiny canoe. Over the next few days, I got to know him quite well. As he opened up, he told me that he was in the last stages of cancer and the doctors had given him about three months to live. Rather than stay in hospital attached to all kinds of tubes, he wanted to live life to the fullest. He was tired of the medications and easily felt exhausted, but he never gave up, not even for a second. To me this was the essence of belief in one's self.

I REALIZED BELIEF CAN INDEED MOVE MOUNTAINS OR AT LEAST, CONQUER THEM. MOMENTS THAT MATTER ARE FEW AND FAR BETWEEN AND ONCE LOST, CAN NEVER BE REGAINED.IN THE RAT RACE OF THE WORLD TODAY, WE TEND TO LOSE OURSELVES AND OUR TRUE PRIORITIES.

Most terminal patients I have met have a very positive attitude. I wondered why that was the case. Is it because life has thrown them into the worst situation and the mind adjusts to deal with it—and the only way is to be positive? Is it that once they hit rock-bottom, there is only one way to go, and that is up? Or is it that a terminal disease puts things into perspective quickly?

When faced with death, one suddenly realizes what the priorities are. Was this what happened to me when I was paralysed suddenly?

What truly matters? We go through life almost always focused on the wrong priorities. Very few people get it right. So if you have two options that feel equally important, which one would you choose? Many years ago, a wise man gave me a simple technique to make this decision. He asked me, 'In five years, which of the two options would you remember?' Try it, it's a very simple but profound technique that always works to keep one's priorities right.

After wishing the wonderful lady from South Africa all the very best, we continued our trek. For the millions of cancer patients in this world, I wanted her to succeed.

By now, we'd been trekking for more than two and a half hours. As we passed the village of Dusa, we were amazed by splendid views of the Taboche peak. Soon we reached the little village of Thokla situated at an altitude 15,200 feet (4,620 metres). Tikka told us that it was our stop for lunch. Lifebuoy looked at his watch and informed us that we had gained about 650 feet (200 metres) in altitude.

The altitude sickness that I had experienced a couple of days ago prompted me to eat well. For no reason, actually, I believed that a good, heavy lunch would prevent such episodes in the future. Tikka told us that there were not a lot of options for food between Thokla and Lobuche. So that was all the more reason for me to make sure that I had a meal. I looked at the menu. I was tired of eating dal-rice twice a day, so I settled on a large bowl of noodle-and-vegetable soup called 'thukpa'. In spite of the bright sun, it was quite cold. My hands were tightly wrapped around the bowl and as the soup went in, my body felt infused with new life.

After my meal, I started to feel a lot better. My muscles were rested and I was feeling a sudden high. I was ready to conquer the next ascent. I am not sure why but that feeling was infectious and the whole team felt the same way. We were done with the food quickly and were ready and packed, raring to get back to our climb. Tikka's surprise was visible.

Despite this enthusiasm, I knew that my body was exhausted and that the energy would deplete soon. But I did not want to lose the high so I spent a few minutes preparing myself mentally for the afternoon session, then stepped out onto the trail.

What we saw before us took the wind out of our excited and energetic sails. Winding up before us was an extremely steep, rocky path. The human mind is frail. Within seconds, our excitement turned to disbelief and despair. What was excitement and the we-can-conquer-the-world attitude a few minutes back had turned into how-can-we-get-through-this-now?

It was definitely a seesaw of emotions. But I had no choice at this point. I was determined not to be a failure. So I put my foot forward and told myself that I would not look up. But that's precisely what my eyes did and what was ahead was a nasty steep gradient full of rocks. I switched to my 100-step rule immediately. But the gradient almost immediately reduced it to a forty-step rule, and then a twenty-step rule soon thereafter. This was perhaps the slowest climb of the entire trip. I was so tired that it took me greater energy to climb over a rock than find a way around it. So that's just what I did.

Besides, I was out of practice in climbing stairs. I had not attempted stair climbing, which would have helped me in my mountain climbing, ever since my back had given way and I had worked my way out of paralysis.

As I made my way up the slope, I was grateful that I had strong knee supports that did not tear into my skin. I was glad at that moment that I had not compromised on quality when I was buying them.

I looked up and the views were spectacular. By now, we'd burnt up all the energy from our lunch, the sun was shining brightly, but the cold winds meant that we faced the old hot–cold conundrum again. The sight of those dazzling mountains, however, made all this effort and pain worth it.

The winds blew harder as the altitude increased, and when they calmed down, I wanted to take off a few layers. Tikka would have none of it, though, saying that the exposure would make me fall sick. So in spite of sweating profusely, I kept the layers on. I figured that it was the price that I had to pay for not falling sick. The distance was not much, but because of the gradient, we took over an hour to reach the plateau at the top. As I walked past the last rock, the ground was flat for a short distance and led to a gate. Beyond it lay the memorial yard, with hundreds of tombstones of the mountaineers who had died on the ascent to the summit. I sat down there for a bit and then walked among the tombstones. One in particular caught my attention. It belonged to someone who had conquered the summit and created a world record by staying there for twenty hours hours continuously. After such a massive accomplishment, it felt ironic that he had fallen and died on his way down. Really, life is fragile. The average life expectancy of humans is about eighty-five years, not even a speck against the backdrop of planet earth. Life is fleeting. Shouldn't we live life every day to its fullest? Moments that matter are few and far between and once lost, can never be regained. Shouldn't we take the time to enjoy and savour the small things, celebrate small victories, and cherish the small achievements? Take the time to celebrate and enjoy life for what it is—a glass always half-full? It is a very simple circle. You do a little, you enjoy it, you do more, and the cycle continues on. It's beautiful. Even the worst situation takes on a mellower hue if you have the right attitude. If you see life as a glass always half-full, it's a lot easier. Easier said than done, I realize. That's BELIEF!

Most people go through life never making a true difference. Here, beneath each tombstone was a person who had died following his or her passion, had courage, fortitude and a desire to do something meaningful with their lives. Hats off to them, and may their souls rest in peace.

As always, Tikka reminded us that we had a long way to go still, and it was time to leave. We made a turn from the memorial yard and immediately got our first look at the Khumbu glacier. This glacier flows down from Mount Everest and eventually melts to become the Doodh Kosi river. We would make the rest of our trip along the glacier. It struck me that we had been following the Doodh Kosi river for eight days and had gained so much altitude that the river was frozen and had become the glacier. I believe in celebrating small victories and this was one of those moments. I had made it to an altitude where the river was always frozen. I let out a loud cheer to celebrate this accomplishment.

The glacier was a magnificent sight to behold. The last time I had seen a glacier was in Patagonia several years ago, and since then, I'd expected all glaciers to be a pristine white. The Khumbu glacier looked like any other mountain—brown, dusty, broken up by a few spots of white. Tikka told us that landslides were a regular occurrence here so the rocks, mud, and debris from the landslides had covered the glacier. Unless you looked carefully, you wouldn't know that it was actually one.

The turn we made along the mountainside and the Khumbu glacier marked the entrance to the Thokla Pass. This meant that we had climbed an elevation of over 800 feet (250 metres) in an hour. The gradient had been steep, but the views had become even more spectacular. Mount Awi looked beautiful, while Mount Lobuche shimmered in the sunrays that

reflected from the lake at its foot. Those who wanted to climb Mount Everest trained on Mount Lobuche, and Tikka pointed out their tents along the lake. I wasn't sure if Tikka meant it when he suggested that we should try it on our way back. Mount Lobuche was almost 20,000 feet (6,000 metres) tall. Given our state of exhaustion and our single goal of getting to the base camp, we were unanimous in ruling that possibility out quickly.

We continued on the trail. The gradient was not too steep, so we made steady progress. Suddenly, the trail stopped and resumed on the other side of the glacier, which meant that we would have to cross the glacier. Walking on ice has never been a pleasure for me. It's a delicate process that takes immense effort, given the slippery nature of the surface. The sun was shining, making the upper layer of the glacier wet, and therefore, even more dangerous. The only way I could make it to the other side was to focus fully on every step I took. The trail narrowed tremendously on the other side. There were hikers coming back, which slowed our progress, as we had to stop for each crossing.

This gave my mind time to wander, and I thought about Anamika's superhuman effort. He'd been suffering from diarrhoea for the last ten days. At lunch, I'd done a simple test to check for dehydration—you pinch the skin on the back of the wrist, pull it up, and then let go. Normally, it will snap back. But Anamika's had taken forever to get back to normal. This meant that he was acutely dehydrated. Even under normal conditions, dehydration can zap a person and make him lifeless. I could not even begin to fathom what Anamika was going through. Yet he was determined to continue. He had complained about being tired and exhausted and the huge dark bags under his eyes were clear indicators that he meant every word of it. But he kept his attitude positive. He never whined and never complained of 'Pappu fever'. He believed he would make it to the base camp and nothing would stop him.

We were above the snow line at this point. The walk along the glacier gave us some beautiful views. Water, ice, and the mountain slopes made the trek an unforgettable experience. Two hours later we reached our camp for the day, Mother's Lodge at Lobouche. We had actually reached 16,500 feet (5,000 metres), the highest altitude I had trekked to in my life.

After a 'bath' and change of clothes, I met the others in the common room. Anamika's dehydration had worsened; he was in pain and had a fever. I got him to lie down and made him drink two litres of water with rehydration medication. Diarrhoea and dehydration go together and can bring a person down as if there

were a ton of bricks weighing on him. We were close enough to feel the destination so there was no way we could stop. I was hoping that he would be okay for the final push tomorrow. The plan was to go straight through to the EBC tomorrow, even if it meant pushing beyond our exhaustion limits. The medicines certainly helped, and I could see the visible change in his face. I was hoping Anamika would be perfect for the big day tomorrow.

At dinner, we met a group from Brazil. They had come halfway around the globe, all the way from São Paulo to trek in Nepal. They were on their way back from the base camp. I asked them about it. They told us that what motivated them to come all the way here were the pristine mountains and their belief in conquering their goals. They'd trekked through various trails for over a month. This made me think again of how rarely we prioritize things that truly matter. Most of the group were successful businessmen. They had decided to take the extended time off, to trek in the Himalayas for a month even if it hurt their business.

In the rat race of the world today, we tend to lose ourselves and our true priorities. The forty-odd active years of our lives when we are in our prime mean we have about 2,000 weekends. If we realized that we were using up 1/2000th of what we have, would we do the same things next weekend? We speak of the work–life balance. Is there truly such a thing? I don't think so. Am I great at managing life? No. Like most people, I struggle, but I know I try really hard.

As I sat sipping my tea, I started thinking of the next day. D-day. The day I had been dreaming off for a long time and had worked so hard to get to. The adrenaline started to pump. I was hoping it was sufficient to get me over the finish line. I was hoping to keep all the pain and exhaustion at bay for the day after. If we attempted to reach base camp tomorrow, I knew it was going to be a very long day, probably the longest so far. But it was moving towards achieving a really long-standing goal and one of the toughest physical challenges I have undertaken in my life, especially after my slipped discs. I expected it to be difficult, but I don't think I would have wanted it any other way. The difficulty would only grant immense satisfaction once we achieved our goal.

EIGHTEEN

DAY NINE
D-Day

DAY NINE DAWNED BRIGHT and early. It was on this day that we hoped to reach our goal. It would be the culmination of years of dreaming and months of planning and practice. But the exhaustion and fatigue could play spoilsport, so there were three possible ways the day could end: 1. We'd make it all the way; 2. We'd make it to Gorakshep, a village at the edge of a frozen lakebed near the Everest, or somewhere in between and stop there; 3. We were not going to make it to even Gorakshep and would have to return disappointed.

Obviously, we were all leaning towards the first option. We were going to try and make it all the way. We were too close to the end to accept defeat at this point. Besides, we were extremely exhausted and not confident that we could push ourselves yet another day after today. So we wanted to do it on this day.

Getting to the EBC from Labouche would mean that we'd go to Gorakshep and push straight ahead to the base camp. Also, once past Gorakshep, there was nowhere else to stop but the base camp. This meant that if we gave up in between, we'd have to return all the way back to Gorakshep for a night halt.

An early start was critical if we were going to make it back before sunset. Labouche was really cold, the coldest we had felt on the trek and the wind had a biting edge to it. Also the fact that the cold had seeped into our bodies over the last eight days made it tougher.

The one thing that was pumping with certainty through all our blood was 'adrenaline'. Adrenaline is what makes our emotions stronger. It makes happiness more intense or stress more real. Life might have been a lot simpler but for this hormone, but of course, equally boring. So I have always nicknamed adrenaline as the 'life is exciting' hormone.

We knew that an early start was critical, and the adrenaline ensured that we did not need an alarm to wake us up. Even though our bodies screamed with pain and fatigue, the excitement levels were zooming high. Our hearts were racing and we were trembling with anticipation. Our minds were ready to make it happen.

Breakfast was quick, and there was a spring in our tired legs. We left Labouche early and were on the trek

EVEN THOUGH OUR BODIES SCREAMED WITH PAIN AND FATIGUE, THE EXCITEMENT LEVELS WERE ZOOMING HIGH. MY BODY JUST QUIT; I COULD NOT MOVE.

by 7 a.m. For once we were ahead of our scheduled time. Considering the distance to be covered today, this turned out to be a blessing. It was so cold that we'd covered every inch of our bodies with multiple layers. The balaclava that I was carrying came in real handy on this morning to fight the winds. Cheering ourselves, we set out on the trail.

We had a 'cannot be defeated' attitude and were vocal about it. I guess the wind must have picked that up. For it started blowing straight at us with a lot of ferocity. This made our progress amazingly difficult, and the wind chill froze my limbs even through all the layers of clothing. Within a few minutes, the excitement died and our attitude changed. Suddenly, it got too much— the hardship, the fatigue, the body pain—and I had to stop. The pressure in my forehead was building up. Anamika joked that it might be a '3-D' day, that I'd need three tablets of my painkiller, 'Dolo', to get through. Ironically, I'd need far more than that.

Progressively, each day had become a 'Dolo day'. We'd been popping them like candy to manage the pain. The normal schedule for me had been two tablets a day, one at lunch and one at dinner before bed. Like any medication, the effectiveness reduced as each day passed by.

I had a Dolo and started back on the trail after a few minutes. We couldn't afford to take it easy today. But the trail from Labouche was steep, my exhausted muscles were refusing to budge, and because of the altitude, breathing got a lot tougher. All this contributed to the fatigue as well. Each new step needed more effort than the last one. Each time the gradient softened, I breathed a little easier and pushed on only to realize that there was a tougher gradient ahead.

As we had gained altitude, nature was shining in all her glory, almost untouched as it was by humans. So it was no surprise that the views were getting better by the minute. All around was the sheer whiteness of the snow and ice. It was as pure as the first snowfall anywhere in the world. It reminded of my days in Kalamazoo, Michigan, when I used to sit in my hot tub in the sun room while it snowed heavily outside. It was one of my small pleasures—watching the snow in the middle of a freezing winter sitting in the warmth of the hot water.

The views of snow and ice enveloping everything in sight were breathtaking. In the distance, we caught a glimpse of the base camp that Tenzing Norgay and Edmund Hillary had set up on their way to the summit back in 1953. Today, the trails were clear and the paths were marked. I could not even fathom what it would have been like for them as they traversed these uncertain terrains with their team. I wondered if I would ever have that kind of courage—the courage to seek the unknown. But what is courage, really? Is it choosing to act despite your fears? Is it strength in the face of pain or grief? Is it standing up for what is right? Or is it simply following your heart?

I am not sure there is a single definition. For the four of us, it was pushing beyond our limits of endurance at that moment.

We stopped to take photographs of the ice caves that were formed by water flowing beneath the frozen ice on top which in turn was covered by the dust from landslides. They were spectacular, and what's more, they gave us a chance to stop and rest. I think we were so exhausted, we were subconsciously slowing down to ease the pain and fatigue. Realizing this, Tikka kept reminding us that we could not afford to be slow, so almost reluctantly, we started making our way forward.

It was a steep winding ascent. We continued to make slow, but steady progress. I was constantly making adjustments to my equipment. I had to do it so often that it was irritating me. My clothes felt as if they weren't comfortable; my poles felt like they were at the wrong height constantly; my shoes didn't seem to find a firm grip. In short, everything was irritating. I paused to ask myself why I was feeling exasperated with myself. That's when I realized that the stress, the gradient, the cold, and the fatigue were all stiffening my back. It felt like the onset of a really bad relapse.

I was glad to see the terrain flatten out. I found a flat rock and placed my equipment on it. In spite of the cold, I removed many layers of my clothing and put them back on, trying to adjust them comfortably. It did not help. I continued to feel annoyed with myself and my back was stiffening. I could feel it, but there was nothing I could do about it. So I decided to push on and deal with it when things got bad.

Past the next winding turn was the gradual descent into Gorakshep. Situated at an altitude of 16,800 feet (5,150 metres), Gorakshep has the beautiful mountains of Lutse and Labouche providing a gorgeous backdrop. Looking at my watch, I realized that we had managed to convert an hour and a half long trek into a three-hour one. We were exhausted and had to stop for a break, so tea and thukpa were ordered. I decided not to wait till the pain was full-blown and had a Dolo.

The sun had been shining brightly all morning. But the temperature was hovering around -10 degrees C, and the strong winds made it even colder. As I sat down on the bench, all my equipment suddenly felt heavy and cumbersome. The fatigue and pain of the last eight days seemed to hit me all at once. I put down all the equipment and peeled off the layers of clothing. As the last piece came off, I realized that my back had given way and soon, I was writhing in pain. It was a sharp, radiating pain that seemed to intensify by the minute. My eyes flooded with tears. I lay down flat on the floor of the tea shop. It was of hard stone and freezing, and soon the cold began to seep into my clothes. I started crying. I had a flashback to two and a half years ago, when I lay in the Emergency room staring at the ceiling. Instead of the chatter of the doctors and nurses running around, it was the sound of trekkers that resonated. But like that day, everything was muted, and all I could see, hear, and sense was my life flashing before me.

I began to panic and cry as memories of the paralysis came flooding back. As if subconsciously, I tried moving my right hand and leg, then breathed a sigh of relief—I could move them. Over the last several months, I had considered this scenario countless times. I had hoped and prayed it wouldn't happened, and prepared myself. But now that it was real, all the preparation had vanished, leaving me with an acute sense of despair.

The pain was intense and not letting off. I was at a point where I couldn't take more pain, but I wasn't sure if painkillers would cause some complication with my blood-thinning medication. I did not know if the altitude and the thin air would have an effect on the medications. I had to choose between giving up the trek and risking an adverse reaction. I chose the latter and popped a couple of strong painkillers.

I was so close to the goal, yet felt so far from it. Would this be added to the long list of unfinished things in my life? The fact that I had reached Gorakshep was not success enough? I cursed the situation. Why did this have to happen at the very end? I had done well so far in holding the pain back. I cried like a baby. I prayed fervently.

I am not sure how long I slept; it must not have been long since the others did not mention it. But it was some of the best few minutes of relaxation I have ever had. In the process, my muscles started to loosen up, and when I woke up, the pain was had lost its edge.

Mentally, I suddenly felt like a million bucks though there was still fear in the back of my mind. It kept reminding me not to take anything for granted.

We had been extremely slow getting to Gorakshep and now we'd lost a lot more time. Could we make it to the base camp and back? We debated this as a team. We were all nervous about whether our bodies could handle another day of such extreme weather and effort. So in spite of the exhaustion and loss of time, we decided to go for it.

Although my pain had not subsided, I decided to go with the flow in the interests of the team. I was hoping that the adrenaline and excitement would mask the pain. I slowly got my gear back on and stepped outside. The pain combined with the cold made this a tough proposition. Patience was the only frame of mind which could keep me going.

As I stepped out, it was bitterly cold and windy. The air felt thin and breathing was difficult, but each step raised our level of excitement. There was nothing left in the tank anymore; it came down to plain determination. The goal felt close. We could sense it.

Tikka told us that it was about an hour and a half's climb to the EBC. If the morning was a benchmark, that meant three hours. Grabbing energy drinks and bars, we started to make our way forward. Most of the trek was through the Khumbu glacier, which meant trekking over ice and snow. As the sun was shining brightly, the surface would be very slippery and we would need to exercise a lot of caution. This also meant that the progress was going to be very slow.

I took each step with immense caution, and this added pressure on my legs and played havoc with my pain. I did not want to speak up lest I dampen the overall mood. I told myself that there was no choice, and that I had to deal with the pain somehow. I tried to distract my mind.

All of us were tired, but kept egging one another on. We'd trekked for about an hour like this, taking several breaks in between. We made a sharp turn along the Khumbu glacier and suddenly, we saw our destination in the distance. Right in front of us was the Everest Base Camp! It felt euphoric. We stopped to capture the moment in many pictures. As the excitement died down, my euphoria gave way to frustration—the valley between us and the base camp was impossible to trek. This meant that we had to continue along the winding path of the glacier. The destination suddenly felt too far away. The pain suddenly felt impossible to handle. My body just quit; I could not move. I sat down.

It was the early hours of the afternoon with only a few hours of sunlight left. We either needed to push forward now or head back to Gorakshep and attempt the route again tomorrow. It was an hour and a half (possibly two with the pain) to the base camp; it was an hour or more to get back. Either way, we had to start moving.

I told myself I was going for it. I stood up although the pain had increased. Telling myself I had no choice, I started back on the trail. The going was tough and slow. We had to stop very frequently to cope with the exhaustion. We kept an eye on our destination, but it did not feel it was getting any closer. A quick look at our watch indicated that we were at an altitude of 17,880 feet (5,450 metres).

As we stopped to capture some of the views on our cameras, we got an unencumbered view of Mount Everest. Fate seemed to be on our side. It was one of those rare days when the peak did not have its normal plume of clouds. Tikka told us that this was an extremely rare sight. As always, we were caught up in the awe of the moment until Tikka pushed us to keep moving.

The pain didn't seem to be getting worse, and I wasn't sure if this was because I was operating on adrenaline now, or if the pain had really plateaued. On a normal day, it would have been enough to keep me in bed. But today was far from normal.

We continued to make slow progress along the edge of the mountain. The trail had become really narrow—avalanches had swept away major pieces of the mountain and also made the air dusty. The narrow trail with the precipitous drop on one side made it treacherous. Tikka wanted to get through this section quickly lest we get caught in an avalanche. He and Ming Ma made us walk between them as a precaution. I was too tired and in too much pain to protest or be adventurous.

I DON'T SEEM TO HAVE A MEMORY OF THAT MOMENT. BUT IT WAS CERTAINLY ONE OF THE BEST MOMENTS OF MY LIFE. I LOST CONTROL OF MYSELF. I BROKE DOWN AND CRIED PROFUSELY.

As I looked past the glacier to the right, the base camp came into view again. I'm sure it wasn't far, but it felt a long distance away. I kept moving forward but the goal didn't feel any closer. The base camp seemed to be at a lower altitude—the trail was descending.

It had been a little over two hours since we had left Gorakshep. Ahead of us was a steep climb up and the base camp was not visible anymore. Tikka informed us that it was just beyond this ascent. I took the comment with a pinch of salt. Tikka was just trying to keep our spirits up. Yet, the hope that this was indeed the last bit got my heart beating fast. At one point, I thought it was so loud that I could almost hear it. With each step, the anticipation grew and the excitement was palpable. It was about a thirty-minute climb. But for the first time, I'd forgotten all about the pain.

I climbed up the last incline and froze. There it was— the Everest Base Camp! I don't really remember what I felt. I was devoid of any emotion or sensation. I don't seem to have a memory of that moment. But it was certainly one of the best moments of my life.

All I can remember is yelling at the top of my lungs. I am not sure what I yelled but I know it was loud. At least it was loud in my mind. I lost control of myself. I broke down and cried profusely. The emotions came flooding in all at once. I was all at once the incapacitated and paralysed man on the hospital gurney making the promise to fight myself out of paralysis and make it to the Everest Base Camp. I was the accomplished leader. I was the scared man that doubted himself. I was the determined man that fought through those doubts. I was choked up. I didn't know what to do, what to say, or how to say it. As I regained some composure and looked around, I realized the entire team was crying. A lot was said though not a single word was uttered.

The reality seemed surreal. We had made it against all odds. We had endured pain, exhaustion, fatigue, and illness, and had won. We had fought hard to keep mind over body and had been successful. At that moment, I was not sure if life could get any better. The language of hugs said all that was to be said. Our lives had changed forever.

For me, the afternoon of April 8 was a far cry from February 12 two years ago in the hospital. It had been the most excruciatingly painful challenge that I had undertaken. From the hospital bed to the base camp—what a long journey it had been! What a roller coaster of emotions, high and low. It had been a path ridden with emotions, pain and the wonders of self-discovery. From the moments of despair to those of exhilaration, from the feelings of being a loser and giving up the fight to pushing myself against all odds and succeeding, it was a journey like no other.

We had made it. Needless to say, we were elated. After we got over the initial euphoria, we took a number of photographs. Individual pictures, group pictures, pictures with flags—all kinds. It was as if we were trying to package our happiness into pictures. I had forgotten the pain. It was afternoon, but time did not seem to matter anymore.

As tradition dictates, we wrote the names of all our loved ones on a Nepali flag and hung it at the Everest Base Camp. My first thoughts were a big thank you to God and all my friends and family for helping to bring me here. I also wrote my name on a big flat stone to let the world know I'd been here. Was it vanity or just plain happiness? At that point, nothing mattered. It was a moment that we wanted to share with the world, especially so with our loved ones. We were literally and figuratively (almost) on top of the world.

It was a moment that was indescribably precious. We lit up the Cuban cigars that we had carried with us. None of us were smokers in daily life, but this occasion warranted a bit of indulgence. As I savoured the moment, euphoria gave way to gratitude. I was truly thankful for our achievement.

The sun was making its way down the horizon and the clouds were scudding in. With the mercury dropping sharply, I plummeted into a steep trough after the high that I had been on for the last half an hour. Like a drug addict, I had reached an ultimate high and so the crash was equally spectacular. The reality of aches, pains and fatigue came surging back.

I wasn't sure how long we had before the sun set. Tikka also realized this and started to push us along. Trekking through narrow icy trails after sunset would not only have been bitterly cold, but treacherous. The trek back to Gorakshep was unusually difficult. We were exhausted emotionally and physically, and even the fact that we were retracing our route back didn't seem to help. With the incentive of reaching the goal now gone, the trail ahead definitely felt like a glass half-empty. Even the initial climb down from base camp felt difficult to navigate.

My back was aching with a vengeance, as if to punish me for the last few hours. About an hour into the trek, the pain became intolerable. I started crying. I felt I wouldn't be able to make it. I just wanted to lie down right there. But fear can be a great motivator. The light was waning and the sun casting longer shadows. I couldn't freeze to death, so I had to fight through the pain and get back to Gorakshep. I stood up. I felt old, and every part of my body felt rusty and stiff. Informing the team that my progress would be very slow, I began walking. It had been a very long day, with over nine hours of trekking already. The mental exhaustion was as pronounced as the physical. It was now a race against the setting sun. I tried to walk as fast as I could, but the sun seemed intent on setting faster. Cursing my pain, I pushed myself even further.

As the last rays of the sun faded away, our lodge at Gorakshep came into sight. With one final push, I walked through its doors, completely frozen and exhausted beyond belief. As I crashed onto the bench in the common room, all I could think of was that I had actually made it to the Everest Base Camp and back. It had been one of the toughest days of my life and one of the best. It had seen the highest of the highs and the lowest of the lows emotionally. This was a day for the books. It was a day that changed my life dramatically.

I was hungry, but I did not feel like eating. I was happy, but I could not smile. I was in so much pain, but I did not have the energy to even cry. The last hour and a half of trekking without the warmth of the sun had frozen my body. I managed to change my clothes and pop a few pills before I collapsed into bed. Gorakshep recorded a bitterly low temperature of -24 degrees C that night. I snuggled under six layers of clothes, inside a liner and sleeping bag, under a blanket, with the hot water bag that Tikka had thoughtfully provided tucked next to me, waiting to get comfortable. But I was so exhausted and in so much pain that sleep eluded me. I lay straight and flat. But I had a smile on my face. As cold, painful, and miserable as it was, it was still aeons away from that warm hospital bed.

NINETEEN

DAY TEN
The descent

WE HAD DONE IT! The four of us. We were four totally distinct individuals who had become one great team. We had pushed and cajoled and driven each other, and over the last nine days, had overcome all odds to achieve our goal. I wondered why it was that each individual's goals, while important, had not been as important as the team goal? Was it that we knew we could not achieve the goal alone? That it would either be all four of us who would succeed or all four who failed? Is that what made us all for one and one for all? When you have common goals, is it easier to accomplish things that would otherwise have been impossible? When do individual goals mean more than the team goals? I was not sure what the answer was. But I sure was grateful that we had one another. With those thoughts, I woke up.

It was to be our first day of our descent. The night had been peaceful and I had woken up with a smile, the sense of accomplishment still reigning supreme. As I tried to stretch myself, the reality came down pretty hard on me. My body was completely bruised and protesting loudly with aches and pains. Realizing I had no choice, I pushed myself out of bed and got moving with the morning chores. The temperature was below freezing and the water was frozen. Hence all activities were abbreviated. The body pain combined with fatigue made everything a drawn-out affair. I crashed on the bed several times before I managed to pack the day bag and the rest of my luggage for the porters. Then I literally dragged myself to the common room for breakfast, where I could only manage to eat a little. A general mood of lethargy prevailed within the team.

Anamika's fever had shot up yesterday and the diarrhoea continued unabated. The medications that he had been taking until now did not seem to have much effect. Since we would begin our descent today, we wouldn't need to take the medicines for altitude sickness, so we decided to overdose him for the fever and diarrhoea hoping that this, along with the lower altitudes, would make him feel a lot better. He was so exhausted that he did not protest or offer an opinion. He just swallowed the pills I gave him like an obedient baby.

With that done, we got on our gear and stepped out. Tikka had told us to expect an easier climb down. From our lodge, it was an initial climb up, and the terrain soon flattened out over the glacier. We were retracing our steps back to Lukla, with no change in the route at all.

I could see the trail on the next mountain at more or less the same height as this one, and I had this hazy idea of building a giant bridge from here to there to avoid the climb down this mountain and up the next one to reach it. As stupid as that thought is, it reflected the state of our minds and bodies. Although we knew there weren't any, we still looked eagerly for shortcuts from Gorakshep to Labouche.

As we trekked, conversation was at an all-time low— we were all lost in our own thoughts. Lifebuoy was walking slightly ahead. He was humming a familiar tune from yesteryears. I decided to catch up with him, and as he started to whistle, I thought of all the conversations that I had with him over the years, and especially the last few days. This macho man had wept when we made it to the base camp and dedicated the achievement to his dad. He believed that his father had been looking after all of us on this trip, giving us ten straight days of sunshine and protecting us at each turn. Making it to the EBC was one of his biggest personal achievements. The trip had made him believe that any adversity can be overcome through faith and determination. That every challenge had a positive angle and was always an opportunity to scale another peak. This adventure had helped him believe in himself much more. As he moved forward in his life, he was certain that irrespective of the issue or situation, the 'I will try' would come loud and clear before the 'I can't do it'.

Lifebuoy was walking with a renewed sense of energy and a spring in his stride. As he started to whistle a very familiar and popular tune, I joined in. Soon the other two joined in as well and within minutes we had split into two teams competing with each other. Once again the mind had won, the aches and pains were put on the backburner, and we sang our way happily down. Time flew fast and before we knew it, we were back in the small village of Labouche and the teahouse where we had spent the night before last.

The singing carried into the teahouse where we sat down to have a cup of tea. Over the course of the morning trek, we had come down almost 1640 feet (500 metres) in elevation. We had managed the ups and downs without realizing that it had taken us over an hour and a half. We decided to keep our tea break at Labouche short and were back on the trail quickly. Tikka wanted to take the lower trail through a small village called Pheriche instead of going through Dingboche. He believed it would be easier on us and we did not object.

The break at the teahouse had exacerbated our fatigue and exhaustion. So the attempt to restart our singing duel did not catch on and we trekked quietly. Naturally, the trek seemed longer with every step. As we came down in altitude, the trek got easier. The air was thicker and hence the breathing got better. The altitude sickness that was playing havoc eased up as well. The temperatures were also getting relatively warmer. It all felt really good.

Though it had a few ascents, the trek down was certainly easier. We had come down almost 3280 feet (1,000 metres) in the morning and the going had been good. When we reached the memorial yard, I paid my respects to the departed and added thank you to God for keeping me safe. The climb down from the memorial yard was steep. But we had our destination for lunch—Pheriche at an altitude of about 14,000 feet (4,300 metres)—in sight throughout. Though the descent was far easier, it was proving to be really tough on my knees. I had to adjust my trekking style and began to rely heavily on my trekking poles. But though it helped ease the pressure on my knees, it aggravated my back pain as it shifted the centre of gravity. After a while and many trials later, I found a style that was easier on both.

From the top of the mountain, I could see Pheriche in the distance. From my vantage point, it seemed close so I started walking briskly. As we trekked in the valley, we were greeted with very strong winds that were blowing right at us because of the 'tunnelling effect'. The temperatures were still very cold, but it was still warmer than Gorakshep, and that made me feel a lot better. Your perspective truly changes depending on where you are.

We had been on the trail for close to five hours, and I was ravenous. I was determined to get to Pheriche as quickly as possible, but the wind had other ideas. It continued to blow hard and strong. Pushing against the wind was exhausting, and made Pheriche seem really far away. Over the last several days, I had learned to accept that the perception of distance in the mountains was not something I could rely on. Yet the frail mind and the exhausted body always had hope that the perception would be the reality. As the winds picked up even more, walking into it felt like I was 'walking up a down escalator'. The trek from Gorekshep to Labouche had set the wrong expectations in our minds. It had made us believe that the descent was going to be easy. Right now, it felt far from it. Once again, it had come down to expectations. I tried to reset my mind and stay focused on the task at hand. All my discipline had gone out the window that morning. I had to remind myself that the descent was almost as tough as the ascent, and I had to get back into the same mode that I had been operating in over the last nine days.

I managed to refocus my mind on the current task and push towards warmth and food. The winds continued strong and unabated. Over the last nine days, we had beautiful sunshine and no wind. I paused for a moment to thank God for the nine glorious days. One afternoon of snowfall in Namche Bazaar had taught us how an entire afternoon could be ruined pretty quickly. Today's winds showed us how hard our trip could have been and almost impossible, in fact, had we not had good weather.

The trek into Pheriche turned out to be one of our toughest. The trail had disappeared and it was now wet and mushy as far as the eye could see. We continued trekking slowly against the wind and had to stop frequently. We finally managed to reach Pheriche and saw that the village was half-a-kilometre long row of small teahouses on either side of a path. Our teahouse was at the very end so this meant trekking another half a kilometre; it felt like 10.

Once we reached the teahouse, I dropped the poles, removed my boots, and lay flat on the surface. I was ravenous, but my back, which had stiffened in the cold, took precedence. Nepali prayers were being played softly in the background. I closed my eyes. I was happy and thrilled. Considering everything, my back had held itself well and I was thankful for it. It had been my biggest fear that it would give way completely and I am glad it was under control.

The hunger and the warmth made the standard dal-rice go down pretty quickly. It felt good as my muscles started to relax. Now that I'd had some food and rest, I looked around. The dining room of this teahouse was different from the others we'd seen so far. To begin with, it was much cleaner. The prayers playing in the background added a sombre, yet calm atmosphere. But because I couldn't understand the language, it felt like the same sentence was repeated over and over again.

The owners had taken time to decorate and add beautiful touches to the room. Many of the trekkers had written notes on their team flags, which had been hung aesthetically from the ceiling. I started reading them and saw they were from all around the world. They spoke about reaching the Everest summit, or reaching the base camp, or somewhere in between. Some were serious, others light-hearted, for example, 'I made it to first base.' Divided as the trekkers were by countries, politics, religion, there was still just one single theme running across all those flags—that of a sense of accomplishment. The essence of the human spirit stayed the same despite all the differences that living in different cultures and countries created. The flags on those walls said just that. Irrespective of the person or the team, the raw human emotion behind the flags was the same. It was humbling to realize that life is far more than the daily grind.

I am human after all. The flags were an ego boost and made me feel good that I could place a flag on that wall if I wanted to. It was a great feeling. At that moment, life certainly was a glass half-full.

**I WAS 'WALKING UP A DOWN ESCALATOR'
I MADE IT TO FIRST BASE. IT WAS HUMBLING
TO REALIZE THAT LIFE IS FAR MORE THAN
THE DAILY GRIND.**

After a long lunch break, Tikka started to push us to get moving. With reluctance, I started back on the trail. Our destination was Pangboche. That meant we had to trek through the valleys of Orsho and Shomare in the afternoon. As usual, we began with a steep climb up. The wind continued to blow straight at us, making the climb more difficult. And just like the other days, we had to plod on—there were not a whole lot of options between Pheriche and Pangbuche.

Eventually, what goes up in life has to come down. And so the steep ascent gave way to a sharp descent into a flat valley. Even better, the wind began to ease up over time. This was a huge relief and made the trek a whole lot easier.

About two hours after our lunch, we reached Pangboche. The weather remained cold, but was a lot less bitter than the last few days. More importantly, because the winds had died down, it felt much warmer than the thermometer indicated. We had come down another 820 feet (250 metres) in altitude. The increasing oxygen levels made it feel much more pleasant.

While I was tired, I still felt like I had energy left in the tank today. A quick change—which was far easier than before—and I was in the common room sipping a cup of tea. The facilities in the teahouses were getting better as we lost altitude. The common room had a new water heater in the middle that I kept eyeing longingly, hoping that the owners would run it. As we relaxed, the exhaustion of the journey hit us hard. The conversation was all about which parts of our bodies were hurting the most and how we were coping with it. For a person listening in from the outside, I am sure it would have sounded like four grumpy old men complaining about the cold and all their bodily aches and pains.

All of a sudden our conversation stopped abruptly. We had seen the hostess approach the heater and our hope that she would start the heater in that cold room perked us up. It was exactly what the doctor ordered at that point. Like my dog drooling over a morsel of food, we were drooling at the prospect of the heat. I was freezing and the hope of warmth got me excited. Looking around, I realized that it wasn't just us—the entire room had fallen silent. All the trekkers were staring at the hostess as she went about starting the heater. It was not an easy process and it took her at least twenty minutes. We waited till it was lit before the next word was uttered.

The normal human expectation of instant gratification kicked in. I had seen the fire lit, so I expected warmth immediately. As if on cue, a big group of Chinese trekkers drew up their chairs all around the heater. I was livid. I had been waiting all this time, and here they were hogging all the warmth. It just did not seem fair. They did not even consider for a moment what they were doing. I wondered if it was just their nature to be selfish.

Sanity prevailed, and I did not protest, but I certainly felt my patience being tested. We asked Tikka to do the 'dirty' job of talking to them but being a soft character, he did not want to do it and asked us to be patient. Patience is definitely a virtue, but for us four weary, exhausted, frozen trekkers it certainly felt like eternity until they moved on and the heater radiated its warmth on us too.

All of us who had commented on their behaviour with righteous indignation proceeded to sit in the very same chairs around the heater that had just been vacated. 'It was cold and we were only four of us; they were ten, and blocked the heater. We at least did not block it fully.' Whatever the lame excuse we came up with to justify our actions, we felt a lot better with the heat seeping into our clothes. As I recollected the incident that night, I was shocked at the frail nature of our minds. When faced with the freezing cold, we had done the same thing that we had criticized others for.

My socks had got wet and I placed my legs on the heater assuming they would dry faster. My legs felt wonderful within a minute, but soon after, I felt something burning. I realized what an idiot I had been. The surface was so hot that it had burned right through my socks. Luckily, I had two pairs on and so only the first pair had burned before I realized it. I guess some things have to take their time—just like my socks.

Another day had passed and we had managed to descend almost 5,000 feet (1,500 metres). It had been a long day and the wind had made it even longer. But the drop in altitude certainly made us more comfortable. It had been a wonderful and satisfying day. I could feel the pressure easing up.

TWENTY

DAY ELEVEN
Surprises and decisions

I HAD SLEPT WELL AND WOKE up in good spirits. The weather was warmer, the air was thicker, and I felt better. More importantly, my back was much more relaxed. We had a choice regarding how far we wanted to trek today. We could take in the sights and stop a short distance away for the night, or we could push ourselves all the way back to Namche Bazaar. For us, Namche Bazaar equated to a warm blanket and a hot shower. Not having bathed in over a week, the incentive was too big to resist. We decided on Namche Bazaar.

A warm shower and warm blanket are among life's simple pleasures. I belong to the privileged lot who take food, shelter, clothes, water, or almost any basics for granted. As I thought about our desire for a simple shower, I remembered that millions go without this daily 'privilege'. I told myself again that I had to learn to cherish the smaller things in life.

We placed our orders for breakfast, and I sent up a quick prayer of thanks that Anamika was finally getting over his sickness. His attitude over the last ten days while suffering from severe diarrhoea and dehydration had been unbelievable. Even with sagging bags under his eyes, he had kept his optimistic smile. All his life he had been a positive person, energetic and motivated. He believed that he was a consummate optimist, unflappable with a strong appreciation for life as it is. He had been truly living his motto of 'living in the moment'. While this had definitely kept him going over the last ten days, it also meant that he had a few regrets that he carried with him always. As I got to know him better, he confessed that there were days he would ponder if he should have pursued an alternate career path, perhaps as an architect (which would have provided a perfect blend of all things that he was passionate about—art, science, and building things) or if he should have joined the armed forces and served his country. He regretted not learning a musical instrument or spending more time with family and friends.

Family means a lot to him. His life today revolves around his work and his wife and son. The trek had been the toughest thing he had ever done physically and mentally and he'd proved to himself that he could accomplish almost anything he set his mind on. This had pushed him to continue smiling through the dehydration and associated symptoms.

My thoughts were disrupted by the arrival of toasts and omelettes. A quick breakfast later, we went off to pack our bags. As I was getting back to my room, my eyes caught MM's. Nothing was said, but both of us felt that same sense of accomplishment. I recalled the time about six months back when I knew him only as a colleague who worked in the same company. We were walking down a hallway to attend a meeting as I talked about the trip and how I was getting a team organized. His ears had immediately perked up and he started barraging me with a million questions. Those were early days and I did not have many answers. At one point when I felt like I could not fudge any more answers and get away with it, I asked him if he wanted to come. Without hesitation came his response: 'Yes, but I need details.' From then to now, it had been quite a journey that both of us were thankful for in more ways than one.

We all gathered in the common room and set out with a smile on our faces. As can be expected, with the declining altitude, there were many more villages dotting the trail. Unlike the previous days, however, the trek did not begin with an ascent. Instead, it was a steep descent to the river. For the eleventh day in a row, the sun shone brightly and the wind was holding back. This made the trek easy and a lot of fun.

Our first destination was the monastery at Tengbouche. We had breathtaking views of the sun reflecting off the fresh snow and ice on the sides of Ama Dablam, or 'mother's lap' in Nepali, and my thoughts went to my mother. The fact that I was enjoying this beautiful trek that morning was because she gave up so much for me. Everything else pales in comparison to a mother's sacrifice. That's when I thought about it—when was the last time I thanked her? I had taken her love and sacrifice for granted. I told myself that I had to call her as soon as I got down and got a signal on my phone. If not, I'd wake up one day and there wouldn't be any more time to do it. That was when I decided to call her every single day of my life for the rest of our lives.

How often do we thank the people who mean the most to us? The ones who put aside everything to help us have a great life? How easy it is to remember people when we need them and forget them as soon as our purpose is served. We have short memories and forget to thank people for all they do for us—family, a friend in the office, a boss. Whether it's a blood relation or a family member like a wife or husband, we forget that the only reason we are who we are is because of what they did for us. We don't attach value to what we have every day. Do we ever thank our bosses who helped us succeed? We never take the time to thank the boss who supported us and sponsored everything we needed to succeed. Even after the person has gone out of your life, do you take a moment to drop a note or call to say 'Thank you'? Humans have been created with the ultimate ability—the ability to love. Unconditional love is rare. In the mad rush of our daily lives, we forget to hold those people close to our hearts only to wake up one day and realize that we have lost a diamond while we were busy collecting stones. As I stared at Ama Dablam, I felt it was the most beautiful mountain I had ever seen. Did its name have anything to do with the way I felt? I am not sure. But it was a meaningful moment and that's all that mattered for me at that time.

We continued our trek down to the valley. With no wind and the trail being all downhill, it took us just an hour of brisk walking to get to the bridge across the river. I stood in the middle of the bridge, staring at the Doodh Kosi flowing rapidly by. The murmuring sound the river created as it wound its way down was so peaceful and serene that it made me pause. I had to soak it in. We were truly in the lap of nature, with nothing to disturb the harmony or spoil it—no loud noises, no sirens, no vehicles, nothing. It was the resounding silence of nature defined by the flowing water and the sound of our breathing.

As we stood on the bridge enjoying the view, we could see the trail ahead of us. The descent continued past the bridge, down the side of another mountain. We were relaxed and stopped frequently to take pictures. As we turned the corner, the trail bottomed out and we were staring at a steep ascent. Tikka told us that this was the final ascent to Tengbouche. The ground had got quite wet from the rain last night and there was also a lot of traffic going the other way. This forced us to walk along the edge of the trail, and that, along with our fatigue, made it tougher. The sudden shift from a relaxed descent to a steep ascent made the going slower and feel longer.

An hour or so of steady climbing brought us to the monastery. We sat down there for a rest, but once again, Tikka reminded us that we had chosen to get to Namche Bazaar, which was still a long way away. Given the lack of time, we decided not to go to the monastery and started back on the trail. Our next stop was Phungi Thanga, where we would have lunch. Phungi Thanga was at an altitude of about 12,200 feet (3,700 metres), a slight descent from where we were currently. That

hardly mattered, because, before every descent, we knew there was a steep and forbidding ascent.

For the first time on the trek, MM was leading the pack. Over the last ten days, he had been trailing, but right now he was well ahead of us. As I stopped to consider this, I realized that he had been in a hurry all day and had been pushing us to move faster. I wondered why this was so. Behind him, we joked that he had all this energy because at last he wasn't constipated. We decided to ask him the reason the next time we took a break, but he kept going at an amazing speed. All of us wanted to reach Namche Bazaar before the end of the day, but we did not want to do it at the expense of missing out on enjoying the trek and causing further harm to our bodies.

Tikka wanted to ensure his safety so he sent Ming Ma forward to keep MM company. We asked Ming Ma to tell MM to stop until we caught up. When we did, we asked him why he was in a mad hurry. His response took all of us by total surprise. He was hoping to reduce our trip by two days so he could get home to his family. His children were in a school play, and if he made it in time, he could watch them on stage.

I wondered if this was a father's love or the same guilt that I had felt a little earlier about my mother.

But it certainly struck a chord with me. He had not expected to be back in time, but now that there was a ray of hope, he wanted to try and reach home on time. He wanted to push further ahead past Namche Bazaar and get to Phakdin today so that we could get to Lukla and leave the following morning.

I was feeling exhausted. I was honest with MM and told him that as much I would love to do it, I wasn't sure I'd be able to. The others felt the same way. He understood what we were telling him, but his mind would not accept it. Holding on to slim hope, he started back on the trail. It was an ascent, and it slowed us down even further. I felt guilty about it, but my legs would not move. I wanted so badly to be back, get a clean shower, some good food, and my bed. I started to miss my mom badly. We continued the trek. Anamika caught up with me and said, 'Can we try and hurry up?' The genuine concern in his voice was evident. I realized immediately that his heart was doing the talking.

Each day had revealed more traits of our characters. Anamika had a strong personality, but a soft heart. His passion for the well-being of the team was evident. He knew we were tired, but he wanted us to try to go faster. I wondered if he was vocalizing the guilt that I was feeling within. My heart responded, 'Sure. Let's try and do this for MM.' I am not sure if I had anything left in the tank, but we were not going to let it go without trying our best to make it happen. Anamika was happy with the response and attitude. In his excitement he started talking. When the mind is happy and heart is pure, the conversations are seamless and wonderful.

The entire conversation felt like a confession. The trip had made Anamika appreciate life much more. His attitude of 'live in the moment' had become cemented even further and stronger. He had always known he was a go-getter. But the trip had confirmed that unless one did something extraordinary, one is bound to become complacent and mediocre. Like with all of us, the trip had taken a toll on him as well. He was emotional and thankful to all of us as a team for pulling him through his weakest moments.

He continued to talk. He sounded like a drunk man speaking with no inhibitions, except he was completely coherent and we had not had a sip of alcohol for over a week. I told myself that this was not the time to interrupt. So I let him carry on talking and responded at appropriate junctures. I was listening with abject attention and, in fact, was quite fascinated. He told me that he has always been a strong believer in karma and had great aspirations to become a multi-millionaire CEO. While he regretted not using his father's influence to move up faster in life, not doing so had given him a strong sense of achievement and satisfaction. All that he was today was because of his hard work. Much of his confidence originated from his belief that he was a self-made man. He knew he could adapt to almost any situation and it was this asset that gave him a very optimistic look into the future. For now, he wanted to live in the moment and nothing more. He was going back home with a much deeper understanding of teamwork, determination, passion, and commitment. He certainly wanted to enjoy the journey of life and not just hurry towards the destination.

Our determination and, therefore, spirits were high. We wanted to make progress so MM could get to his goal. But our bodies were just not keeping up. We tried in vain, but the going continued to be slow. We felt dejected and desperate.

Was it karma? Was it God continuing to be kind to us—for the eleventh day in a row? I am not sure. But as if on cue Tikka walked up to us with a surprise! He asked us if we wanted to take a helicopter from Namche Bazaar to Lukla. There was one that was returning that afternoon and could accommodate us.

I believe it was the exhaustion—Tikka's question just passed by my brain without registering. I kept wondering what I could do to speed up our descent as Anamika and I continued our trek. At least ten minutes must have passed before we looked at each other as if struck by a lightning bolt. Here was the answer to the problem that we had been wrestling with! The chopper ride would serve two purposes. It would completely round up the experience, and more importantly, give MM a chance to be with his kids for their annual day function. What were we thinking? What was there to deliberate? We took the decision and told Tikka to make arrangements. We were taking the chopper back to Lukla.

Friendship is probably one of the best manifestations of human behaviour. Friendship is as old as mankind. While there are millions of ways to define friendship, what sums it up all for me is the quote: 'A true friend is not one who bails you out of jail but is in jail with you for the same crime'. It's often said, friendships forged on battlefields are the strongest kind in the world. Eleven days in the mountains through emotional highs and lows forged a strong bond among us four that I think will last a lifetime. We leaned on one another when we were exhausted. We shared with one another when we were happy. We pulled one another up. We were always there for one another through thick and thin.

Since I had been on the road most of my professional life and, therefore, missed out on a lot of my daughter's childhood, I felt really close to MM's emotional state. So trying to help him would truly give me happiness and joy. The other two felt the same way and agreed that it would be a wonderful gesture on our part. What is it about surprises that make the gift or event even more wonderful? A surprise birthday party or get together, a surprise ending? While there can be bad surprises at times, the general sentiment associated with the word is positive. As I thought more about it, I realized people who plan a surprise enjoy it as much as the ones that are surprised. This was one such occasion. I suggested that we keep quiet and not let MM know about the plan till the very end. The others immediately agreed. We all experienced a sudden rush of excitement. After all, the scheming and planning is always the fun part of the surprise.

My initial thought was not to raise his hopes because the helicopter ride had many caveats. The first was that we had to get to Namche Bazaar by 2 p.m. That meant we had to shave off almost an hour and a half from our original plan. We were not sure we could manage that. The other problem was that the helicopter could not wait for us. And critical to our plans was the weather, which, in the mountains, was highly unpredictable and could change in a matter of

a few minutes. The fact that it was sunny currently meant nothing. From what we had seen, it was usually clear in the mornings and got extremely cloudy in the afternoons. This meant that we did not have a strong chance of getting on that helicopter.

But there was still a chance, and for MM's sake, we were going to give it a shot. I prayed that the elements would cooperate and kept my fingers crossed that we could achieve yet another goal that we had set for ourselves, one that came with a lot of emotions and hence passion.

Suddenly, I had a spring to my step. I told myself that I was indeed a slave to goals. In my case, I need a definitive goal to pursue, whether it is personal, professional, or emotional. At that moment, the fact that I had a target with the promise of being emotionally enriching made easier. I realized that my mind was indeed frail and the more I learnt to control it the better I would deal with life.

We really wanted to try and so pushed ourselves hard. We made really good progress and reached the village of Phungi Thanga located in the valley between Tengbouche and Namche Bazaar. We had come down to an altitude of about 11,000 feet (3,350 metres). Although we wanted to continue and make it to Namche on the slim chance that we could get the chopper, we were really famished and needed to eat. So we decided to break for lunch at Phungi Thanga.

Sitting there together waiting for the food, it dawned on me that this was possibly the last meal together on this trek. I was all choked up. A lot had changed since we started on this trek—I had changed too, and I realized that I did not want return to that daily grind, that rat race that was once my life. The last ten days had given me serenity and I did not want to give that up.

The sun was shining brightly into the sun room that we were in. Life seemed as bright and the secret that we were holding from MM was adding to the excitement. The altitude was lower and the air was significantly thicker. My body was feeling a lot better with the added oxygen. I was hungry and had to go in for second helpings.

We had decided to not reveal the surprise till the very last moment possible. In order to build up the drama of the situation even more, we tried to tease MM. He was quite desperate and was trying to hurry us up at every step. While we were eating as fast as we could, we pretended not to care too much about his desperation. We even had an artificial vote as to who was interested in getting to Phakdin that

night. Other than MM, all of us deliberately voted against. MM's growing anger and frustration was visible. However, he remained silent and this lack of response to the bait was frustrating. I attributed MM's lack of response to the fact that he was totally oblivious to our devious plans and hence went with the flow rather than think too much of it. Either way, the camaraderie, the affection, and the excitement in the air that day is what I'll carry with me forever as a memory of true friendship.

After lunch, I suggested we all stay together. That meant I did not want MM to pick up from where he left off that morning and start running ahead. I asked him to stay back with us. While he did not know why I said that, he was a team player and agreed immediately.

I looked at my watch. It was 12.30 p.m. That meant that we had ninety minutes to reach Namche Bazaar. I looked over at Tikka enquiringly and he responded that it was a ninety-minute trek normally. If the last eleven days were any indication, that meant a two-and-a-half-hour trek for us. Tikka added the caveat that it was a further twenty minutes to the helipad.

I suddenly felt bad. We had been building up the excitement with the hope that we would make it to the chopper on time. With the last bit of information from Tikka, our chances of making it to the chopper by 2 p.m. had diminished. I felt a little disappointed in Tikka. Had he told us this before, we might have hurried up even more or even picked up something on the go rather than sit down for lunch. But then I could have asked him before lunch, which I never did. So I was partially to blame as well. Irrespective of who was to blame, the situation was what it was. It reminded me of what my father had taught me. With any problem, there are two choices. If you know the solution and can do something about it, start working towards it. If circumstances are beyond your control and you can't do anything about it, why worry?

The weather had warmed up and the trail was mostly in good condition. The trek from Phungi Thanga to Namche Bazaar is through the beautiful valley of Khumjung. As if the stars fell in place for us, the trail was almost all downhill, which made the trek much easier. This, combined with our determination meant that we were making strong and steady progress. The decline ensured that we did not have to take breaks either. At points, we were jogging as fast as our heavy trekking boots would allow. It looked like we were not going to miss the chopper. The weather or any multitude of reasons could play spoilsport, but it sure wasn't going to be us.

As it happens often in the mountains, the bright sunshine abruptly changed to clouds and it started snowing. Within a span of fifteen minutes, it had become cold and wet. My momentum was cut in half as snow pellets started to hit me. However, this did not dampen my spirits. I had a goal, and I wanted to make it by 2 p.m. I was doing this for MM. This was our last trek. It would take a lot more than snow to slow me down. I told myself that any resulting pain could be dealt with later.

At times, we were almost sprinting. The trail was thankfully more or less flat, and so the small ups and downs on the trail did not really affect our pace. It stopped snowing and the sun started shining brightly. My thoughts drifted to the day I met MM for the first time. He was sitting across my desk being interviewed for his current job. My first impressions were of a young man who seemed to have an air of calm self-confidence about him, one that I was sure was the result of success achieved through hard work. Needless to say, I was impressed. He joined the firm shortly thereafter and as I got to know him better, I realized that he had grown up in a family where graduating from high school was considered a major achievement. He had made it against the odds, working hard at every juncture. He had moved up in life without guidance or a mentor, but that only meant that though he made mistakes, he learnt from them and then corrected them.

He was a consummate family man, devoted to being a good son, and committed to being an excellent father and husband. One day over drinks, when we were discussing love, he remarked, 'I was married before I found love. I discovered it post marriage and it has been the most wonderful thing in my life.'

Over the last several years, he had felt the urge many times to do a 'lot more' to make up for 'lost' time. I asked him if that was just the normal mid-life crisis. To which he smiled and responded, 'Maybe. As I look back, I am happy. God has been kind to me. My life might not have been perfect, but it has been great in many ways.' For me, this statement summed up his character. He was neither an optimist nor a pessimist. Life had taught him to be a realist. He had tried hard to do the best he could under any given circumstance, whether it was helping establish a charity for the education of the underprivileged or training to be a private pilot.

MM believes that he can be defined by the words 'love', 'joy', and 'adventure'. While he regretted not living up to his potential in these areas, the trek to the EBC had revitalized his spirit of adventure. In the last eleven days, it had become an extension

of love and joy. It had firmed up his belief that he could accomplish almost anything he set his mind to. While his priorities had not changed, the manner in which he wanted to accomplish them certainly had. He had tried keeping a journal on the trip. As he looked at it, he realized that most of what he had written revolved around his family. That had reset and helped prioritize his goals.

My thoughts were interrupted by the sight that greeted us as we made the sharp turn to the right around the mountain. It was the beautiful crescent-shaped bowl of Namche Bazaar. I looked at my watch. We had made it in sixty-five minutes. That meant that we had twenty-five minutes to spare. After eleven days, for the first time, we had done it faster than Tikka had predicted. I was thrilled that we had actually arrived in time for the helicopter and that MM had a chance of being home for his kids.

Tikka pointed out the clearing where the helipad was located. But MM and Ming Ma were already ahead of us. Ming Ma, being in on the plan, had stopped short of Namche Bazaar, much to MM's chagrin. When we caught up, I could see the annoyance on MM's face. He had not received a satisfactory explanation from Ming Ma regarding why they were waiting. It was a perfect setting for us to break the surprise.

We had been carrying the surprise for several hours and it was now reaching a crescendo—we all were bursting at the seams to divulge it. We had been planning all the way. The camera was ready and so was I. To keep the suspense, I pretended it was a regular interview for my video journal similar to those I had done every single day of the trek, so he was cornered. I deliberately kept the questions vague and long-winded. With every question, he grew more and more impatient. I think every person in the group, including Tikka and Ming Ma, enjoyed this. All except MM. I am sure he knew something was up—we were all suppressing chuckles and smiles—he just couldn't put his finger on it. So when MM looked like he was about to quit talking, that was my cue. I told him that we were going to be airborne in the next thirty minutes and he would get home in ample time for his kids' annual function.

We waited in anticipation for his reaction. We waited, and then some more, but he just didn't react at all. I repeated the whole thing to him again, assuming he hadn't heard me the first time around. Still nothing. The others chimed in and tried to clarify and rephrase my statements—but he just stood there. We had been building the excitement for four hours in our heads and this was the worst let-down.

My immediate guess was that he already knew and was playing all of us, doing a damn good job at holding a smile back. I was truly impressed. Why had I not anticipated this? Had the other two also been in on this joke? One look at their faces showed that they were equally baffled by MM's lack of response.

We laughed nervously, gazing at MM. His expression had not changed at all. Suddenly, I was worried and asked him directly about what he was feeling. After a lot of cajoling, he confessed that he thought we were pulling yet another prank on him. I felt bad, and I am sure the others felt the same. Had we done this so often that he did not trust us at all? I joked that we must have been really good pranksters and for the first time, MM smiled, albeit guardedly.

All of us continued to explain our actions over the last several hours—that for once we weren't teasing him. Slowly, as the minutes ticked by, I got the sense that he was actually considering the possibility of the 'joke' being real. I realized we could not get him to believe it fully until we reached the helipad and were on board. In all this excitement, we had lost a lot of time. So we were back to hurrying.

The route to the helipad was from Namche Bazaar. But that would mean a long hike into the valley and then a climb up to the helipad. We decided to take a shortcut and try our luck on the edge of the mountainside. As we started walking away from Namche Bazaar, MM slowly began to believe that the chopper plan was actually real. But he didn't want to get excited lest the excitement was short-lived and there was another twist to the tale. When he finally cracked a genuine smile I knew he'd accepted that we were hoping to get a ride out today.

He was trekking with me, and for a moment, I thought he would cry. He looked at me and said 'thank you'. For me, personally, those were among the best words that I had ever heard in my life. He thanked all of us multiple times. He started to say something more, but not many words came out—he was so overwhelmed by our gesture. He did not have to say a word. I knew exactly what he was trying to say. Tears were flowing freely. With our overwhelming exhaustion and body pain, there was no easy way to stop the stream of tears.

What had happened in the last four to five hours was a befitting end to a wonderful journey. Several months ago, we had embarked on this journey with a willingness to share and support one another in everything. We had done just that and had made it against all odds. I could see that MM was shocked and surprised and felt on top of the world. He, like all of us, was high on the excitement and emotion of the moment.

As we trekked off the trail towards the helipad, he told me that this trip had meant a lot to him, and that he was extremely thankful that he had undertaken it. It had given him an opportunity to step away from the rat race and reflect on what truly matters. That in the last eleven days he had seen joy, love, and adventure—three words that he believed was reflective of his character—in full measure, and that he hoped to live a life in which he'd find all three in abundance.

As he spoke, I choked up as well. I am not sure if it was what he said, or the moment, or the circumstances that played out, the happiness of the trip, or the exhaustion and pain, or simply everything put together. I did not want to think about the why. All I know is that it turned out to be exactly what I had hoped for—one of the most precious moments of the trip.

We struggled to find a path that we could actually trek through to get to the helipad, and that meant our progress was slow, which made us nervous. After all the effort that we had put in to get here on time, it would be too much if we missed the helicopter. Tikka tried to reassure us in his classic style, telling us that we were almost there.

The sun was on its journey down and lit the beautiful bowl of Namche Bazaar up with sweeping rays of sunshine. It was a sight like no other, and one that I probably will never witness again.

We tried to hurry up as fast as the path would allow and our legs would move. The helipad was a small area that had been cut into the mountainside to make it flat, and we were one uphill climb away from it. Though the distance wasn't much, climbing over bushes and rocks made it tough, and it was with my last reserves of energy that I finally walked through the gates of the helipad area. My watch showed 1.59 p.m. We had made it with one minute to spare.

That afternoon, I had tapped into some stockpile of energy I didn't even know existed. It had given me irrefutable proof that the mind and the body are linked in more ways than we know of. The last eleven days had cemented this fact in my mind as I was the living, breathing proof of the power of the mind.

The trip was a goal that we had all been emotionally vested in for a long time. Helping MM achieve something he wanted to was also a goal I was committed to. While I was physically exhausted, my passion to achieve my goals had somehow been able to tap into energy reserves from deep within. This has been the story of my life.

I walked across the helipad and stood close to the rocks forming the boundary; beyond this was the steep mountainside. It was a moment to pause and reflect on the last twelve days. The reality was sinking in. I had done it. The sense of accomplishment sent a shiver down my spine. The hard work had paid off. The countless prayers had resulted in the miracle.

I have always felt that life is a privilege. Success has not come automatically to me, and I have had to work hard for it each time. I grew up as an academically average kid in school. My childhood was marred with asthma, a chronic condition that ensured I missed most of my classes, and physically, grew up well behind my age group. This meant that I was at the receiving end of all the abuses and pranks of every bully and even the 'wannabe bullies'. This stage of my life could explain a lot of my character today. The countless times of cowering and hiding behind a bush or crying against a lonely school wall and swearing to seek revenge some day might have shaped the person that I am. The strong willpower and determination that I have today is probably to combat the deep-seated fear of the next bully around the corner. I have wondered if the confidence that I have today is a reflection of the success I have had or an overcompensation to mask the fear within.

At that moment, though, life seemed like the glass half-full. But it was life. Nothing is permanent nor lasts forever. Over my right shoulder, I saw ominous clouds move in and my hopes began to crash. Mouthing a small prayer, I walked over to the team who were busy taking pictures. I joined the fun and even went on to capture the last video journal of the trip.

With the clouds darkening, the hope of the helicopter coming that afternoon to pick us up was fast diminishing. But strangely, that did not dampen my spirits. I had made it to the EBC and back against all odds and life was still wonderful. The sight of a beautiful eagle soaring majestically against the backdrop of the spectacular mountains lifted my spirits. I prayed a little more. As if my prayers seemed to have received an immediate response, the winds picked up and started to blow the clouds away. I then bounced back up again. I guess the roller coaster of life never changes and is dimensionless, even if ups and downs are two-dimensional.

The good news about being down is that there is only one way to go—up—and it will happen sooner than later. I was still surprised at myself for having managed to get to the helipad that afternoon. At first, I had no hope that we would make it, only that it felt emotionally right to try. Because I knew I was doing the right thing, I was passionate about it and I had trekked with a prayer in my heart. Climbing the mountains had felt a lot easier. Each time the pain had cropped up, I'd reminded myself of what it meant for MM.

There is no doubt that many physical disorders and other related symptoms like an upset stomach, anger, anxiety, loneliness, or depression, are induced by emotions. Physical symptoms are a direct result of the strong feelings that are repressed in the unconscious part of our brains. That being a fact, I wondered if the reverse were true as well. Could an emotion induce physical pain? There are innumerable instances of people displaying extraordinary strength or superhuman feats under seemingly impossible conditions and even in dire circumstances, which shows that willpower can conquer any odds.

While our circumstances weren't dire and nor was it a superhuman feat, I wondered if I had forgotten the pain and exhaustion that afternoon as a result of repressed emotions in the brain that were positive. I had gone from a hopeless physical state to not only making it to the helipad, but doing so with time to spare.

As I looked at the sun making its way down to the horizon, I had just one thought in my mind. I had done it! It was a wonderful feeling. With the state my back was in, I had not been sure I could make it to the Everest Base Camp. While I believed in myself and had the determination and passion, the lingering doubt had always been there. And the fear of failure had been ever present.

In everyday life, I had tended not to do what I really wanted to because of my fear of failure. We seldom stop to consider what failure truly is. Is it not being able to achieve the final result or is it not even attempting to do something? If I had not reached the EBC, if I had succumbed to pain at Gorakshep and returned, would that the trip have been a failure? As has been said, 'Don't be a collector of bad wines. If the opportunity is right and the person is right, open it'.

A little doubt and fear is very healthy. It helps us achieve what we set our minds to. It's the butterflies in the stomach, the tiny beads of perspiration before we have to take an exam that impel us forward. The fear of failure was a big part of the story of this trek for me. As I stood on the ledge, I realized that the fear that had been lessening each day since I made it to the top was gone. It had been a triumph for four amateurs with little training to have climbed to such heights and back successfully. It was a moment to realize that life is wonderful.

I TOLD MYSELF AGAIN THAT I HAD TO LEARN TO CHERISH THE SMALLER THINGS IN LIFE FRIENDSHIP IS PROBABLY ONE OF THE BEST MANIFESTATIONS OF HUMAN BEHAVIOUR I HAD CHANGED TOO, AND I REALIZED THAT I DID NOT WANT RETURN TO THAT DAILY GRIND, THAT RAT RACE THAT WAS ONCE MY LIFE

My professional career has been quite successful so far. Many that have seen my rise in the ranks might conclude that I have achieved it all through precise calculation and action. The truth is the exact opposite. I have gone with the flow. Whenever an opportunity has presented itself, I have taken it. Almost always I have got into roles that I did not know a lot about, but worked hard to learn once I was there. Hard work and undying loyalty has been my motto. There are many things in life that I regret, from giving up studying medicine to not spending enough time with my daughter as she was growing up. The list is quite long, but what mattered to me at this point was that I have a great deal to be thankful for.

Suddenly, from around the mountain, I heard the sound of a helicopter. This meant that the weather had cleared—the chopper service was operational and coming to pick us up. We could get our ride to Lukla today. As it hovered over the helipad, my excitement grew. Set against the background of the glaciers flowing down from the mountains, the chopper came towards us.

As the helicopter landed and the sound of its blades died down, the silence of the mountains felt deafening. We loaded our luggage and got in. It was a tight fit with six people on board, including Tikka and the pilot. Then, at last, we were in the air. We flew through the valley with beautiful awe-inspiring mountains on each side. It was indeed a different view than from the top of the trail. We flew over rivers and villages and soon landed in Lukla. I looked at my watch—it had taken about fifteen minutes. It had made a very short trip of a two-day trek. I felt for a moment that it had trivialized our trek as, on reflection, a helicopter ride could not give us the enjoyment and experience that the trek had. But the ride offered as our last views of the spectacular Himalayas from a vantage-point that couldn't be matched by views from the ground. It rounded up our experiences for sure.

We landed in Lukla at the helipad just off the runway. It was afternoon, and there were no flights between Lukla and Kathmandu at that time. All flights between the two cities were in the morning only because the cloud cover typically thickens in the afternoon, and

given the perilous nature of the Lukla airport, none of the airlines wanted to take the risk of operating in the afternoon. So that meant we were going to spend the night at Lukla. We checked in at a teahouse and got to our rooms. We rested our weary bodies for a while and then got back together in the common room.

That evening was the most relaxed one in the last twelve days. All accounts were settled. While we laboured to carry ourselves up and down, the Sherpas had carried all our luggage each day. To us, they were the heroes. As much as one can argue that it is what they do every day of their lives and/or it's their livelihood, it is really hard work. So we tipped them and also gave them all the extra food we had not consumed. They were extremely happy with the tips and I think the extra food was the clincher.

We were still at around 9,000 feet (2,700 metres) but the air, though cold, was easier to breathe in. I am sure psychologically we were in a lot better place. Realizing that we had to wake up for a very early flight the next day, we went to bed. For the first time in several days, we did not have to sleep in iceboxes. Some layering and a thick blanket was what I finally settled on. Sleep came quite easily and quickly.

THE FINAL CHAPTER
The end...a beginning

THE NIGHT BELONGED TO SEVERAL stray dogs that were barking loudly and fighting with each other. So my sleep was limited to the first three hours after I went to bed. All of us found ourselves wide awake, except Anamika, who had finally managed to recover from all his ailments, and with multiple beers in him, slept through the loud, tumultuous night.

I overheard voices from the adjacent room and decided to join Lifebuoy and MM, who had also woken up to the noise. We spent the rest of the night chatting about the trip and a whole lot more. The last twelve days were fast becoming memories.

The crack of early dawn was on us and the weather looked clear. So assuming the flights would be on schedule, we woke Anamika up and after our morning chores, we packed up and were ready to head for the airport. In spite of the good weather, the flight schedules were unpredictable. So we decided to grab some breakfast, lest we got stuck at the airport for a long time.

The Sherpas got our big bags to the airport while we walked on with our backpacks. It was a short walk, but it gave me a chance to once again reflect on the help they and Tikka had given us. This trip would not have been possible without them for sure. We had reached the base camp and had pictures to prove it— starting tomorrow, we would share them with all our friends and family. We would receive all the accolades for the accomplishment, for one journey. Would we ever think of the Sherpas and guides who do this every day? Even when Sir Edmund Hillary climbed the Everest along with Sherpa Tenzing Norgay, they had over 300 people to carry their luggage, food, and other equipment. Nowhere in history are any of them documented or acknowledged. They are truly the unsung heroes. We had struggled our way to the top, while each porter had carried two of our 15-kilogram bags each and still managed to go much faster than us each day. We may say their bodies are accustomed to the gruelling climbs, the terrain, and the altitudes as regular climbers, but if we think about it, their resilience and endurance is amazing.

Thanks to Tikka's experience, we got through the formalities, such as check-in and security, expeditiously in spite of the chaos of the Lukla airport. Soon, we could hear the sound of the first plane coming in, and this was followed by several others. All the planes came in, landed, and stopped at the very end of the runway where the airport building was located. Similar to Kathmandu, it felt like a bus terminal. Luggage was unloaded, passengers got off, passengers got on, their luggage was loaded, and the plane was ready to take off. The turnaround was so quick that the pilots did not even bother to turn the engines off.

The Phakdin Four had made it. We were physically bruised and were covered with cuts, aches, and pains. I had not showered for almost ten days now, and I felt dirty. I hadn't felt this way when I was in the mountains, but all of a sudden I felt extremely unclean. I was really looking forward to getting to our hotel in Kathmandu and jumping in the shower.

To the outside world, I am a strong, successful, determined, passionate individual. Someone who knows what I want and not fearful about finding a way to achieve it. The truth is I am the most indecisive person ever. My strong will and determination is in a constant battle with an extremely soft, emotional side. Each time I have gone with the flow, seized an opportunity, and made something out of the opportunity. However, the indecision has caused me some trouble and resulted in many regrets. I want to be the best in everything I do, but I also want to spend the rest of my life in a shack on the beach with no worries of the world. I want to go back and be an entrepreneur because I feel that is in my blood, but need to curb the fear of the work and effort needed. I want to run a marathon in less than three hours, but the excuses to not to do so are too many. I could fill a book with all that I want to do and have not done.

It had been a tough journey to the Everest Base Camp and back, mentally more than physically. As I thought about it, I felt emotional. The God that I believed in had helped me all the way. In my adopted home of the United States, there is a tradition called 'Thanksgiving'. While I had nothing to do with the first Pilgrims who arrived in the US as immigrants, I love 'Thanksgiving' for the fact that it's the one time in a year when we pause and give thanks for what we have in life. As I stood there by the window, looking at the planes, and thanked God, I was grateful for my dream to trek up to the Everest Base Camp after my paralysis, and the circumstances and the support I had to achieve it. I was glad I had the strength to overcome the pain, the ability to see the beauty in life, and most importantly, the attitude to fight through and pursue one of the most difficult endeavours that I had undertaken to date.

It had been a humbling experience. The mountains were indeed a wonderful leveller. It reminded me of the old adage, 'Whether you are a common man or the president—you still have to put on your pants one leg at a time'.

I was thankful to the team, the Phakdin Four. We had worked and functioned as an amazing team. Our camaraderie had kept us going; each of us had taken strength from the others. I am positive I could not have done it without them. We had forged a deep bond of friendship in the battle against physical and mental adversity and the elements.

I felt a lot of gratitude for my family and friends who supported us over the last several months through every step.

It had been a great trip. It was not necessarily the magnificence of the mountains or the gorgeous valleys, or even the trek; what made it special was

the mental peace. For the first time in decades, I had actually disconnected completely from work and felt a sense of freedom for over twelve days. On all previous vacations or weekends, I'd at least checked my email, if not done more than that. To be without the Internet or network connectivity in the mountains was a wonderful blessing. In the mountains, the addiction to electronic gadgets and all things digital was also broken. Conditioned as I was to connectivity, I still had the undying tendency to put my hand in my pocket and pull out my cell phone. But when I'd got back to office after the break in the mountains, I realized that life does not end without the Internet or the office, or work, or gadgets.

As we'd trekked through the mountains, many thoughts had crossed my mind. I wondered if the yogis and sages of yesteryears had mastered the realities of life, and that's why they'd found peace. When one meditates in peace one realizes that roses are indeed beautiful if you take the time to smell them. I have talked about the rat race many times. The mountains had the soothing effect of cancelling that white noise and giving my mind much-needed peace.

Over the course of the trek, I'd realized one of the biggest truths of life: that the mind is more powerful than anyone can fathom. I managed to accomplish something that I could not have dreamt of a couple of years ago. The mind can perform miracles, using the body as a tool, even if it doesn't cooperate.

Almost every single day, my body had given up. The trek was the most excruciatingly difficult thing I'd attempted. My muscles had been screaming with pain all the time, and with the bitter cold and its attendant challenges, quitting had been an easy option. The body could not handle itself at many points on the trek. It was the mind that had worked overtime to keep moving forward. It was a strange realization that the mind could overcome almost anything that the body could not.

As we'd walked and trekked and climbed, our conversations had ranged from the serious to light-hearted banter to the outright ridiculous. Hearing my friends talk, I realized is that everyone has their own problems in life. Not just one or two but plenty. Each person feels and believes that their problems are the worst. Each person works out the best possible solutions to handle the problems they face.

One hears many sayings and quotes, but push it to the backburner and move ahead. For me, one saying makes sense, 'It does not matter what hand you are dealt with in life each day. What matters is what you do with it.' Chance and luck might have a say in circumstances that confront one, but ultimately the person's ability to cope to deal with difficulties and problems is what brings peace of mind.

For once I had done something that I would remember for the rest of my life. When I stood on the bridge over the Doodh Kosi, all my priorities over the last few years had flashed before me. It had been work, work, and more work. But as I tried to discern exactly what I did, each day seemed to be the same as the previous one or the one after, each day blending into the next. It begged the question of whether I had done anything that truly mattered. If I couldn't remember what I did a few years ago, did it even count? I realized then that I have to reprioritize and do what matters. When faced with choices, I should focus on what I would remember fondly two, three, five years from now. It was a wonderful feeling and I felt a lot lighter. A refreshing breeze had blown across my face suddenly as if life was giving me a sign that said 'Thumbs up!'

This trip had been about tremendously hard work and perseverance and a strong sense of determination.

Goals and targets change in shape and size with individuals. As is often said, 'If you can achieve it, you have not dreamt big enough'. There is never a perfect answer. But having something to look forward to, whatever it is, drives you and motivates you. Common sense would tell you that being 'aimless' does not go too far. Even if you believe you are chilling out, that's a goal because your goal is to relax. If you think you don't want to do anything, well, that's a goal as well. It might not get you anywhere, but certainly fits the definition.

I have always believed in dreaming big. My mother always told me, 'Reach for the stars so you will at least get to the moon.' Great things have been achieved in this world by people who have dared to dream big. Don't accept anything as impossible. Set yourself a target that is beyond your immediate reach and work towards it.

'IT IS NOT THE MOUNTAIN THAT I CONQUERED, IT IS MYSELF'. THE ONLY THING THAT KEPT ME GOING WAS 'ATTITUDE'

Discipline is a word that is almost always attached to hard work. As amateurs, we needed focus and discipline to get to the top. Many parts of the trek were treacherous and could have proven fatal. We needed the discipline to be organized and committed, to be determined at all stages. Plenty of obstacles were thrown at us—aches, pains, cuts, bruises, highs, lows, smiles, tears. It took determination and grit to hold on and accomplish what we did.

The sense of accomplishment made up for anything we had to give up on. It was truly satisfying. Standing there at the Everest Base Camp felt like a million bucks and some more.

Those twelve days were truly a life-changing experience for me. I had the time and the environment for intense introspection and gave me the biggest sense of accomplishment I have ever had.

I thank everyone and everything that helped me get to the Everest Base Camp. As Clarence Hodges remarked, 'For today and all its blessings, I owe the world an attitude of gratitude.'

If I were to sum up the entire experience, it would come down to one word—attitude. Every step of the way, life is all about attitude. As I look at it, life is a blessing and always a glass half-full.

Our plane arrived and we boarded. As we took off from the tiny airstrip at Lukla, I told myself I was not going to let life be just what happens to me—I would make plans and seize each moment as if it were the last one. Carpe diem!

I know I had a renewed sense of determination, a renewed sense of vibrancy, and a definite feeling of accomplishment. From being paralysed and helpless lying in the hospital gurney to the top of the Everest base camp...

NOTE ON THE AUTHOR

Hari Kumar is a Managing Partner with Deloitte LLP and is an entrepreneur with a history of growing businesses across US and Asia. He is a strategist and a global, multi-cultural organization and business-builder with a track record of establishing, leading and growing businesses and companies. An exceptional leader, motivator and innovative thinker with a focus on the importance of 'ownership' of your life, your work, your firm and your people and the work they do to enable the development of leaders in an inclusive and socially responsible culture. Author and speaker in leading business magazines and conferences of the world; Motivational speaker; Board member for major charitable institutions.

Hari has been featured in several U.S., Indian and global magazines and newspapers. He was named as 'one of the top 50 Indian entrepreneurs in the U.S.' by Silicon India magazine and as 'one of hottest young executives in India' by *Business Today*. The Forum for Women in Leadership (WILL) honoured Hari with the WILL Women's Choice

Award for 2011, in recognition for his contribution to the mission and mandate for leveraging the vast talent pool of women, creating an enabling and inclusive environment in the workplace, mentoring women for leadership positions, and driving balanced leadership in corporate India.

Hari has authored several articles and white papers on technology, business, motivation and leadership. His latest white paper on entrepreneurship titled 'Fear of failure: Entrepreneurship sclerosis in organizations' has received numerous accolades in the market. Hari speaks regularly at major industry conferences, events and leading business schools around the world on a variety of topics ranging from current and future of IT/ITES companies to trends in the telecommunications industry. He is also a recognized motivational speaker on a wide range of topics including leadership.

As part of his commitment to the community, Hari supports several charities including running an orphanage for girls in Hyderabad, India. Hari serves on the founding board of United Way of India and serves on the Boards of Junior Achievement India and Junior Achievement Worldwide Asia Pacific.

A sports enthusiast, Hari is an avid runner, mountaineer and golfer.